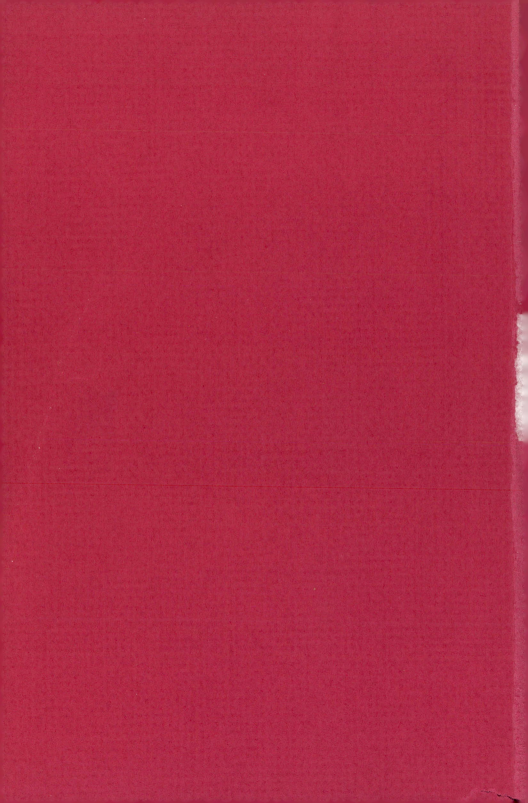

TRANSFORMATIONS

To the Challenge
May it last a
long time
Shari

TRANSFORMATIONS

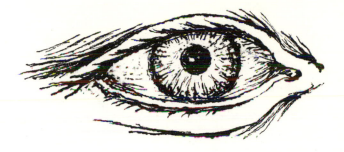

BY ANNE SEXTON

WITH DRAWINGS BY
BARBARA SWAN

HOUGHTON MIFFLIN COMPANY
BOSTON

Second Printing H

Some of the poems in this volume have previously ap-
peared in the following magazines: *Audience*: "Iron
Hans" and "The Maiden Without Hands"; *Cosmopoli-
tan*: "Snow White and the Seven Dwarfs" and "Hansel
and Gretel"; *Playboy*: "The Little Peasant"

ISBN: 0-395-12721-1
Library of Congress Catalog Card Number: 71-156489
Printed in the United States of America

To LINDA,
who reads Hesse
and drinks clam chowder

FOREWORD

by Kurt Vonnegut, Jr.

"Death starts like a dream, full of objects and my sister's laughter," Anne Sexton says in another book. "We are young," she goes on, "and we are walking and picking wild blueberries all the way to Damariscotta."

God love her.

. .

I asked a poet friend one time what it was that poets did, and he thought awhile, and then he told me, "They extend the language." I thought that was neat, but it didn't make me grateful in my bones for poets. Language extenders I can take or leave alone.

Anne Sexton does a deeper favor for me: she domesticates my terror, examines it and describes it, teaches it some tricks which will amuse me, then lets it gallop wild in my forest once more.

She does this for herself, too, I assume. Good for her.

. .

I don't know her well. I met her at a party for Dan Wakefield, a mutual friend. Dan had just published a novel about the tacky and bleak love life of a young man in Indianapolis after the Korean war. She had written a lot of love poems, I knew. One of them began like this:

This is the key to it.
This is the key to everything.
Preciously.

I am worse than the gamekeeper's children,
Picking for dust and bread.
Here I am drumming up perfume.

Let me go down on your carpet,
your straw mattress — whatever's at hand
because the child in me is dying, dying.

It is not that I am cattle to be eaten.
It is not that I am some sort of street.
But your hands found me like an architect.

Jugful of milk! It was yours years ago
when I lived in the valley of my bones,
bones dumb in the swamp. Little playthings.

And so on. There wasn't any woman as alive and appreciative as all that in Dan's book about Indianapolis. I, too, was from Indianapolis.

Indianapolis, by the way, is the world's largest city not on a navigable waterway.

. .

So I tried to be delightful to Anne Sexton, and a lover of life (which I'm not), and I drew for her this diagram of the story of Cinderella:

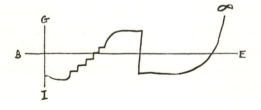

"G" was good fortune. "I" was ill fortune. "B" was beginning. "E" was end. Cinderella was low at the start. She sank even lower when her rotten stepsisters went to the party and she stayed home.

Then her fairy godmother appeared, gave her a dress and glass slippers and a carriage and all that. The steps in my chart represented those donations of valuable merchandise. Cinderella went to the party, danced with the prince. She crashed at midnight, but she wasn't as low as she used to be — because she remembered the party.

Then the glass slipper fit her, and she married the prince. She became infinitely happy forever — which includes now.

.   .

And I learn just now from an encyclopedia, which my wife bought volume by volume from a supermarket, that I graphed the English version of the story, which was translated from Charles Perrault's telling of it in French.

I learn something more from the encyclopedia, and I would have enchanted Anne Sexton and everybody at the party with it, if only I'd known: in the process of translation, the word *vair* was mistaken for *verre* so that Cinderella's fur slippers became glass.

So much for lucky poetry.

.   .

Anne Sexton found it kinky that I should tell her about Cinderella, since she was then absorbed by a darker, queerer version of that story — by the Brothers Grimm. She was, in fact, retelling many of the Grimms' fairy tales in poetry.

And here they are.

So much for mental telepathy. So much for new friends.

. .

How do I explain these poems? Not at all. I quit teaching in colleges because it seemed so criminal to explain works of art. The crisis in my teaching career came, in fact, when I faced an audience which expected me to explain *Dubliners* by James Joyce.

I was game. I'd read the book. But when I opened my big mouth, no sounds came out.

CONTENTS

TRANSFORMATIONS

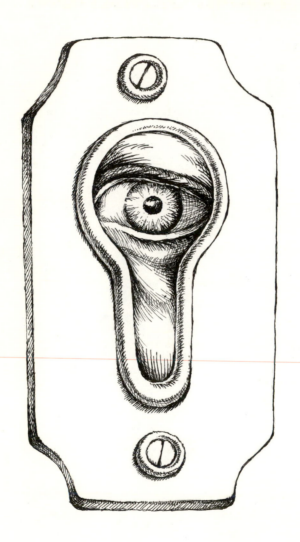

THE GOLD KEY

The speaker in this case
is a middle-aged witch, me —
tangled on my two great arms,
my face in a book
and my mouth wide,
ready to tell you a story or two.
I have come to remind you,
all of you:
Alice, Samuel, Kurt, Eleanor,
Jane, Brian, Maryel,
all of you draw near.
Alice,
at fifty-six do you remember?
Do you remember when you
were read to as a child?
Samuel,
at twenty-two have you forgotten?
Forgotten the ten P.M. dreams
where the wicked king
went up in smoke?
Are you comatose?
Are you undersea?

Attention,
my dears,
let me present to you this boy.
He is sixteen and he wants some answers.
He is each of us.
I mean you.
I mean me.
It is not enough to read Hesse
and drink clam chowder
we must have the answers.
The boy has found a gold key
and he is looking for what it will open.
This boy!
Upon finding a nickel
he would look for a wallet.
This boy!
Upon finding a string
he would look for a harp.
Therefore he holds the key tightly.
Its secrets whimper
like a dog in heat.
He turns the key.
Presto!
It opens this book of odd tales
which transform the Brothers Grimm.
Transform?
As if an enlarged paper clip
could be a piece of sculpture.
(And it could.)

SNOW WHITE
AND THE SEVEN DWARFS

No matter what life you lead
the virgin is a lovely number:
cheeks as fragile as cigarette paper,
arms and legs made of Limoges,
lips like Vin Du Rhône,
rolling her china-blue doll eyes
open and shut.
Open to say,
Good Day Mama,
and shut for the thrust
of the unicorn.
She is unsoiled.
She is as white as a bonefish.

Once there was a lovely virgin
called Snow White.
Say she was thirteen.
Her stepmother,
a beauty in her own right,
though eaten, of course, by age,
would hear of no beauty surpassing her own.
Beauty is a simple passion,

3

but, oh my friends, in the end
you will dance the fire dance in iron shoes.
The stepmother had a mirror to which she referred —
something like the weather forecast —
a mirror that proclaimed
the one beauty of the land.
She would ask,
Looking glass upon the wall,
who is fairest of us all?
And the mirror would reply,
You are fairest of us all.
Pride pumped in her like poison.

Suddenly one day the mirror replied,
Queen, you are full fair, 'tis true,
but Snow White is fairer than you.
Until that moment Snow White
had been no more important
than a dust mouse under the bed.
But now the queen saw brown spots on her hand
and four whiskers over her lip
so she condemned Snow White
to be hacked to death.
Bring me her heart, she said to the hunter,
and I will salt it and eat it.
The hunter, however, let his prisoner go
and brought a boar's heart back to the castle.
The queen chewed it up like a cube steak.
Now I am fairest, she said,
lapping her slim white fingers.

Snow White walked in the wildwood
for weeks and weeks.
At each turn there were twenty doorways
and at each stood a hungry wolf,
his tongue lolling out like a worm.
The birds called out lewdly,
talking like pink parrots,
and the snakes hung down in loops,
each a noose for her sweet white neck.
On the seventh week
she came to the seventh mountain
and there she found the dwarf house.
It was as droll as a honeymoon cottage
and completely equipped with
seven beds, seven chairs, seven forks
and seven chamber pots.
Snow White ate seven chicken livers
and lay down, at last, to sleep.

The dwarfs, those little hot dogs,
walked three times around Snow White,
the sleeping virgin. They were wise
and wattled like small czars.
Yes. It's a good omen,
they said, and will bring us luck.
They stood on tiptoes to watch
Snow White wake up. She told them
about the mirror and the killer-queen
and they asked her to stay and keep house.
Beware of your stepmother,

they said.
Soon she will know you are here.
While we are away in the mines
during the day, you must not
open the door.

Looking glass upon the wall . . .
The mirror told
and so the queen dressed herself in rags
and went out like a peddler to trap Snow White.
She went across seven mountains.
She came to the dwarf house
and Snow White opened the door
and bought a bit of lacing.
The queen fastened it tightly
around her bodice,
as tight as an Ace bandage,
so tight that Snow White swooned.
She lay on the floor, a plucked daisy.
When the dwarfs came home they undid the lace
and she revived miraculously.
She was as full of life as soda pop.
Beware of your stepmother,
they said.
She will try once more.

Looking glass upon the wall . . .
Once more the mirror told
and once more the queen dressed in rags
and once more Snow White opened the door.

This time she bought a poison comb,
a curved eight-inch scorpion,
and put it in her hair and swooned again.
The dwarfs returned and took out the comb
and she revived miraculously.
She opened her eyes as wide as Orphan Annie.
Beware, beware, they said,
but the mirror told,
the queen came,
Snow White, the dumb bunny,
opened the door
and she bit into a poison apple
and fell down for the final time.
When the dwarfs returned
they undid her bodice,
they looked for a comb,
but it did no good.
Though they washed her with wine
and rubbed her with butter
it was to no avail.
She lay as still as a gold piece.

The seven dwarfs could not bring themselves
to bury her in the black ground
so they made a glass coffin
and set it upon the seventh mountain
so that all who passed by
could peek in upon her beauty.
A prince came one June day
and would not budge.

He stayed so long his hair turned green
and still he would not leave.
The dwarfs took pity upon him
and gave him the glass Snow White —
its doll's eyes shut forever —
to keep in his far-off castle.
As the prince's men carried the coffin
they stumbled and dropped it
and the chunk of apple flew out
of her throat and she woke up miraculously.

And thus Snow White became the prince's bride.
The wicked queen was invited to the wedding feast
and when she arrived there were
red-hot iron shoes,
in the manner of red-hot roller skates,
clamped upon her feet.
First your toes will smoke
and then your heels will turn black
and you will fry upward like a frog,
she was told.
And so she danced until she was dead,
a subterranean figure,
her tongue flicking in and out
like a gas jet.
Meanwhile Snow White held court,
rolling her china-blue doll eyes open and shut
and sometimes referring to her mirror
as women do.

THE WHITE SNAKE

There was a day
when all the animals talked to me.
Ten birds at my window saying,
Throw us some seeds,
Dame Sexton,
or we will shrink.
The worms in my son's fishing pail
said, It is chilly!
It is chilly on our way to the hook!
The dog in his innocence
commented in his clumsy voice,
Maybe you're wrong, good Mother,
maybe they're not *real* wars.
And then I knew that the voice
of the spirits had been let in —
as intense as an epileptic aura —
and that no longer would I sing
alone.

In an old time
there was a king as wise as a dictionary.
Each night at supper

a secret dish was brought to him,
a secret dish that kept him wise.
His servant,
who had won no roses before,
thought to lift the lid one night
and take a forbidden look.
There sat a white snake.
The servant thought, Why not?
and took a bite.
It was a furtive weed,
oiled and brooding
and desirably slim.
I have eaten the white snake!
Not a whisker on it! he cried.
Because of the white snake
he heard the animals
in all their voices speak.
Thus the aura came over him.
He was inside.
He had walked into a building
with no exit.
From all sides
the animals spoke up like puppets.
A cold sweat broke out on his upper lip
for now he was wise.

Because he was wise
he found the queen's lost ring
diddling around in a duck's belly
and was thus rewarded with a horse

and a little cash for traveling.
On his way
the fish in the weeds
were drowning on air
and he plunked them back in
and the fish covered him with promises.
On his way
the army ants in the road pleaded for mercy.
Step on us not!
And he rode around them
and the ants covered him with promises.
On his way
the gallow birds asked for food
so he killed his horse to give them lunch.
They sucked the blood up like whiskey
and covered him with promises.

At the next town
the local princess was having a contest.
A common way for princesses to marry.
Fifty men had perished,
gargling the sea like soup.
Still, the servant was stage-struck.
Nail me to the masthead, if you will,
and make a dance all around me.
Put on the gramophone and dance at my ankles.
But the princess smiled like warm milk
and merely dropped her ring into the sea.
If he could not find it, he would die;
die trapped in the sea machine.

The fish, however, remembered
and gave him the ring.
But the princess, ever woman,
said it wasn't enough.
She scattered ten bags of grain in the yard
and commanded him to pick them up by daybreak.
The ants remembered
and carried them in like mailmen.
The princess, ever Eve,
said it wasn't enough
and sent him out to find the apple of life.
He set forth into the forest for two years
where the monkeys jabbered, those trolls,
with their wine-colored underbellies.
They did not make a pathway for him.
The pheasants, those archbishops,
avoided him and the turtles
kept their expressive heads inside.
He was prepared for death
when the gallow birds remembered
and dropped that apple on his head.

He returned to the princess
saying, I am but a traveling man
but here is what you hunger for.
The apple was as smooth as oilskin
and when she took a bite
it was as sweet and crisp as the moon.
Their bodies met over such a dish.
His tongue lay in her mouth

as delicately as the white snake.
They played house, little charmers,
exceptionally well.
So, of course,
they were placed in a box
and painted identically blue
and thus passed their days
living happily ever after —
a kind of coffin,
a kind of blue funk.
Is it not?

RUMPELSTILTSKIN

Inside many of us
is a small old man
who wants to get out.
No bigger than a two-year-old
whom you'd call lamb chop
yet this one is old and malformed.
His head is okay
but the rest of him wasn't Sanforized.
He is a monster of despair.
He is all decay.
He speaks up as tiny as an earphone
with Truman's asexual voice:
I am your dwarf.
I am the enemy within.
I am the boss of your dreams.
No. I am not the law in your mind,
the grandfather of watchfulness.
I am the law of your members,
the kindred of blackness and impulse.
See. Your hand shakes.
It is not palsy or booze.
It is your Doppelgänger

trying to get out.
Beware . . . Beware . . .

There once was a miller
with a daughter as lovely as a grape.
He told the king that she could
spin gold out of common straw.
The king summoned the girl
and locked her in a room full of straw
and told her to spin it into gold
or she would die like a criminal.
Poor grape with no one to pick.
Luscious and round and sleek.
Poor thing.
To die and never see Brooklyn.

She wept,
of course, huge aquamarine tears.
The door opened and in popped a dwarf.
He was as ugly as a wart.
Little thing, what are you? she cried.
With his tiny no-sex voice he replied:
I am a dwarf.
I have been exhibited on Bond Street
and no child will ever call me Papa.
I have no private life.
If I'm in my cups
the whole town knows by breakfast
and no child will ever call me Papa.
I am eighteen inches high.

I am no bigger than a partridge.
I am your evil eye
and no child will ever call me Papa.
Stop this Papa foolishness,
she cried. Can you perhaps
spin straw into gold?
Yes indeed, he said,
that I can do.
He spun the straw into gold
and she gave him her necklace
as a small reward.
When the king saw what she had done
he put her in a bigger room of straw
and threatened death once more.
Again she cried.
Again the dwarf came.
Again he spun the straw into gold.
She gave him her ring
as a small reward.
The king put her in an even bigger room
but this time he promised
to marry her if she succeeded.
Again she cried.
Again the dwarf came.
But she had nothing to give him.
Without a reward the dwarf would not spin.
He was on the scent of something bigger.
He was a regular bird dog.
Give me your first-born
and I will spin.

She thought: Piffle!
He is a silly little man.
And so she agreed.
So he did the trick.
Gold as good as Fort Knox.

The king married her
and within a year
a son was born.
He was like most new babies,
as ugly as an artichoke
but the queen thought him a pearl.
She gave him her dumb lactation,
delicate, trembling, hidden,
warm, etc.
And then the dwarf appeared
to claim his prize.
Indeed! I have become a papa!
cried the little man.
She offered him all the kingdom
but he wanted only this —
a living thing
to call his own.
And being mortal
who can blame him?

The queen cried two pails of sea water.
She was as persistent
as a Jehovah's Witness.
And the dwarf took pity.

He said: I will give you
three days to guess my name
and if you cannot do it
I will collect your child.
The queen sent messengers
throughout the land to find names
of the most unusual sort.
When he appeared the next day
she asked: Melchior?
Balthazar?
But each time the dwarf replied:
No! No! That's not my name.
The next day she asked:
Spindleshanks? Spiderlegs?
But it was still no-no.
On the third day the messenger
came back with a strange story.
He told her:
As I came around the corner of the wood
where the fox says good night to the hare
I saw a little house with a fire
burning in front of it.
Around that fire a ridiculous little man
was leaping on one leg and singing:
Today I bake.
Tomorrow I brew my beer.
The next day the queen's only child will be mine.
Not even the census taker knows
that Rumpelstiltskin is my name . . .
The queen was delighted.

She had the name!
Her breath blew bubbles.

When the dwarf returned
she called out:
Is your name by any chance Rumpelstiltskin?
He cried: The devil told you that!
He stamped his right foot into the ground
and sank in up to his waist.
Then he tore himself in two.
Somewhat like a split broiler.
He laid his two sides down on the floor,
one part soft as a woman,
one part a barbed hook,
one part papa,
one part Doppelgänger.

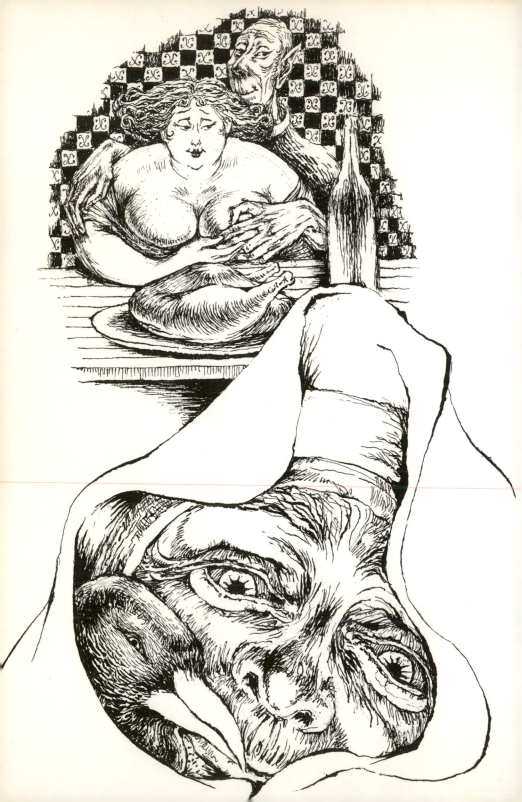

THE LITTLE PEASANT

Oh how the women
grip and stretch
fainting on the horn.

The men and women
cry to each other.
Touch me,
my pancake,
and make me young.
And thus
like many of us,
the parson
and the miller's wife
lie down in sin.

The women cry,
Come, my fox,
heal me.
I am chalk white
with middle age
so wear me threadbare,
wear me down,

wear me out.
Lick me clean,
as clean as an almond.

The men cry,
Come, my lily,
my fringy queen,
my gaudy dear,
salt me a bird
and be its noose.
Bounce me off
like a shuttlecock.
Dance me dingo-sweet
for I am your lizard,
your sly thing.

Long ago
there was a peasant
who was poor but crafty.
He was not yet a voyeur.
He had yet to find
the miller's wife
at her game.
Now he had not enough
cabbage for supper
nor clover for his one cow.
So he slaughtered the cow
and took the skin
to town.
It was worth no more

than a dead fly
but he hoped for profit.

On his way
he came upon a raven
with damaged wings.
It lay as crumpled as
a wet washcloth.
He said, Come little fellow,
you're part of my booty.

On his way
there was a fierce storm.
Hail jabbed the little peasant's cheeks
like toothpicks.
So he sought shelter at the miller's house.
The miller's wife gave him only
a hunk of stale bread
and let him lie down on some straw.
The peasant wrapped himself and the raven
up in the cowhide
and pretended to fall asleep.

When he lay
as still as a sausage
the miller's wife
let in the parson, saying,
My husband is out
so we shall have a feast.
Roast meat, salad, cakes and wine.
The parson,

his eyes as black as caviar,
said, Come, my lily,
my fringy queen.
The miller's wife,
her lips as red as pimentoes,
said, Touch me, my pancake,
and wake me up.
And thus they ate.
And thus
they dingoed-sweet.

Then the miller
was heard stomping on the doorstep
and the miller's wife
hid the food about the house
and the parson in the cupboard.

The miller asked, upon entering,
What is that dead cow doing in the corner?
The peasant spoke up.
It is mine.
I sought shelter from the storm.
You are welcome, said the miller,
but my stomach is as empty as a flour sack.
His wife told him she had no food
but bread and cheese.
So be it, the miller said,
and the three of them ate.

The miller looked once more

at the cowskin
and asked its purpose.
The peasant answered,
I hide my soothsayer in it.
He knows five things about you
but the fifth he keeps to himself.
The peasant pinched the raven's head
and it croaked, Krr. Krr.
That means, translated the peasant,
there is wine under the pillow.
And there it sat
as warm as a specimen.

Krr. Krr.
They found the roast meat under the stove.
It lay there like an old dog.
Krr. Krr.
They found the salad in the bed
and the cakes under it.
Krr. Krr.

Because of all this
the miller burned to know the fifth thing.
How much? he asked,
little caring he was being milked.
They settled on a large sum
and the soothsayer said,
The devil is in the cupboard.
And the miller unlocked it.
Krr. Krr.

There stood the parson,
rigid for a moment,
as real as a soup can
and then he took off like a fire
with the wind at its back.
I have tricked the devil,
cried the miller with delight,
and I have tweaked his chin whiskers.
I will be as famous as the king.

The miller's wife
smiled to herself.
Though never again to dingo-sweet
her secret was as safe
as a fly in an outhouse.

The sly little peasant
strode home the next morning,
a soothsayer over his shoulder
and gold pieces knocking like marbles
in his deep pants pocket.
Krr. Krr.

GODFATHER DEATH

Hurry, Godfather death,
Mister tyranny,
each message you give
has a dance to it,
a fish twitch,
a little crotch dance.

A man, say,
has twelve children
and damns the next
at the christening ceremony.
God will not be the godfather,
that skeleton wearing his bones like a broiler,
or his righteousness like a swastika.
The devil will not be the godfather
wearing his streets like a whore.
Only death with its finger on our back
will come to the ceremony.

Death, with a one-eyed jack in his hand,
makes a promise to the thirteenth child:
My Godchild, physician you will be,

the one wise one, the one never wrong,
taking your cue from me.
When I stand at the head of the dying man,
he will die indelicately and come to me.
When I stand at his feet,
he will run on the glitter of wet streets once more.
And so it came to be.

Thus this doctor was never a beginner.
He knew who would go.
He knew who would stay.
This doctor,
this thirteenth but chosen,
cured on straw or midocean.
He could not be elected.
He was not the mayor.
He was more famous than the king.
He peddled his fingernails for gold
while the lepers turned into princes.

His wisdom
outnumbered him
when the dying king called him forth.
Godfather death stood by the head
and the jig was up.
This doctor,
this thirteenth but chosen,
swiveled that king like a shoebox
from head to toe,
and so, my dears,
he lived.

Godfather death replied to this:
Just once I'll shut my eyelid,
you blundering cow.
Next time, Godchild,
I'll rap you under my ankle
and take you with me.
The doctor agreed to that.
He thought: A dog only laps lime once.

It came to pass,
however,
that the king's daughter was dying.
The king offered his daughter in marriage
if she were to be saved.
The day was as dark as the Führer's headquarters.
Godfather death stood once more at the head.
The princess was as ripe as a tangerine.
Her breasts purred up and down like a cat.
I've been bitten! I've been bitten!
cried the thirteenth but chosen
who had fallen in love
and thus turned her around like a shoebox.

Godfather death
turned him over like a camp chair
and fastened a rope to his neck
and led him into a cave.
In this cave, murmured Godfather death,
all men are assigned candles
that inch by inch number their days.

Your candle is here.
And there it sat,
no bigger than an eyelash.
The thirteenth but chosen
jumped like a wild rabbit on a hook
and begged it be relit.
His white head hung out like a carpet bag
and his crotch turned blue as a blood blister,
and Godfather death, as it is written,
put a finger on his back
for the big blackout,
the big no.

RAPUNZEL

A woman
who loves a woman
is forever young.
The mentor
and the student
feed off each other.
Many a girl
had an old aunt
who locked her in the study
to keep the boys away.
They would play rummy
or lie on the couch
and touch and touch.
Old breast against young breast . . .

Let your dress fall down your shoulder,
come touch a copy of you
for I am at the mercy of rain,
for I have left the three Christs of Ypsilanti,
for I have left the long naps of Ann Arbor
and the church spires have turned to stumps.
The sea bangs into my cloister

for the young politicians are dying,
are dying so hold me, my young dear,
hold me . . .

The yellow rose will turn to cinder
and New York City will fall in

before we are done so hold me,
my young dear, hold me.
Put your pale arms around my neck.
Let me hold your heart like a flower
lest it bloom and collapse.
Give me your skin
as sheer as a cobweb,
let me open it up
and listen in and scoop out the dark.
Give me your nether lips
all puffy with their art
and I will give you angel fire in return.
We are two clouds
glistening in the bottle glass.
We are two birds
washing in the same mirror.
We were fair game
but we have kept out of the cesspool.
We are strong.
We are the good ones.
Do not discover us
for we lie together all in green
like pond weeds.
Hold me, my young dear, hold me.

They touch their delicate watches
one at a time.
They dance to the lute
two at a time.
They are as tender as bog moss.

They play mother-me-do
all day.
A woman
who loves a woman
is forever young.

Once there was a witch's garden
more beautiful than Eve's
with carrots growing like little fish,
with many tomatoes rich as frogs,
onions as ingrown as hearts,
the squash singing like a dolphin
and one patch given over wholly to magic —
rampion, a kind of salad root,
a kind of harebell more potent than penicillin,
growing leaf by leaf, skin by skin,
as rapt and as fluid as Isadora Duncan.
However the witch's garden was kept locked
and each day a woman who was with child
looked upon the rampion wildly,
fancying that she would die
if she could not have it.
Her husband feared for her welfare
and thus climbed into the garden
to fetch the life-giving tubers.

Ah ha, cried the witch,
whose proper name was Mother Gothel,
you are a thief and now you will die.

However they made a trade,
typical enough in those times.
He promised his child to Mother Gothel
so of course when it was born
she took the child away with her.
She gave the child the name Rapunzel,
another name for the life-giving rampion.
Because Rapunzel was a beautiful girl
Mother Gothel treasured her beyond all things.
As she grew older Mother Gothel thought:
None but I will ever see her or touch her.
She locked her in a tower without a door
or a staircase. It had only a high window.
When the witch wanted to enter she cried:
Rapunzel, Rapunzel, let down your hair.
Rapunzel's hair fell to the ground like a rainbow.
It was as yellow as a dandelion
and a strong as a dog leash.
Hand over hand she shinnied up
the hair like a sailor
and there in the stone-cold room,
as cold as a museum,
Mother Gothel cried:
Hold me, my young dear, hold me,
and thus they played mother-me-do.

Years later a prince came by
and heard Rapunzel singing in her loneliness.
That song pierced his heart like a valentine
but he could find no way to get to her.

Like a chameleon he hid himself among the trees
and watched the witch ascend the swinging hair.
The next day he himself called out:
Rapunzel, Rapunzel, let down your hair,
and thus they met and he declared his love.
What is this beast, she thought,
with muscles on his arms
like a bag of snakes?
What is this moss on his legs?
What prickly plant grows on his cheeks?
What is this voice as deep as a dog?
Yet he dazzled her with his answers.
Yet he dazzled her with his dancing stick.
They lay together upon the yellowy threads,
swimming through them
like minnows through kelp
and they sang out benedictions like the Pope.

Each day he brought her a skein of silk
to fashion a ladder so they could both escape.
But Mother Gothel discovered the plot
and cut off Rapunzel's hair to her ears
and took her into the forest to repent.
When the prince came the witch fastened
the hair to a hook and let it down.
When he saw that Rapunzel had been banished
he flung himself out of the tower, a side of beef.
He was blinded by thorns that pricked him like tacks.
As blind as Oedipus he wandered for years
until he heard a song that pierced his heart

like that long-ago valentine.
As he kissed Rapunzel her tears fell on his eyes
and in the manner of such cure-alls
his sight was suddenly restored.

They lived happily as you might expect
proving that mother-me-do
can be outgrown,
just as the fish on Friday,
just as a tricycle.
The world, some say,
is made up of couples.
A rose must have a stem.

As for Mother Gothel,
her heart shrank to the size of a pin,
never again to say: Hold me, my young dear,
hold me,
and only as she dreamt of the yellow hair
did moonlight sift into her mouth.

IRON HANS

Take a lunatic
for instance,
with Saint Averton, the patron saint,
a lunatic wearing that strait jacket
like a sleeveless sweater,
singing to the wall like Muzak,
how he walks east to west,
west to east again
like a fish in an aquarium.
And if they stripped him bare
he would fasten his hands around your throat.
After that he would take your corpse
and deposit his sperm in three orifices.
You know, I know,
you'd run away.

I am mother of the insane.
Let me give you my children:

Take a girl sitting in a chair
like a china doll.
She doesn't say a word.

She doesn't even twitch.
She's as still as furniture.
And you'll move off.

Take a man who is crying
over and over,
his face like a sponge.
You'll move off.

Take a woman talking,
purging herself with rhymes,
drumming words out like a typewriter,
planting words in you like grass seed.
You'll move off.

Take a man full of suspicions
saying: Don't touch this,
you'll be electrocuted.
Wipe off this glass three times.
There is arsenic in it.
I hear messages from God
through the fillings in my teeth.

Take a boy on a bridge.
One hundred feet up. About to jump,
thinking: This is my last ball game.
This time it's a home run.
Wanting the good crack of the bat.
Wanting to throw his body away
like a corn cob.
And you'll move off.

Take an old lady in a cafeteria
staring at the meat loaf,
crying: Mama! Mama!
And you'll move off.

Take a man in a cage
wetting his pants,
beating on that crib,
breaking his iron hands in two.
And you'll move off.

Clifford, Vincent, Friedrich,
my scooter boys,
deep in books,
long before you were mad.
Zelda, Hannah, Renée.
Moon girls,
where did you go?

There once was a king
whose forest was bewitched.
All the huntsmen,
all the hounds,
disappeared in it like soap bubbles.
A brave huntsman and his dog
entered one day to test it.
The dog drank from a black brook;
as he lapped an arm reached out
and pulled him under.
The huntsman emptied the pool
pail by pail by pail

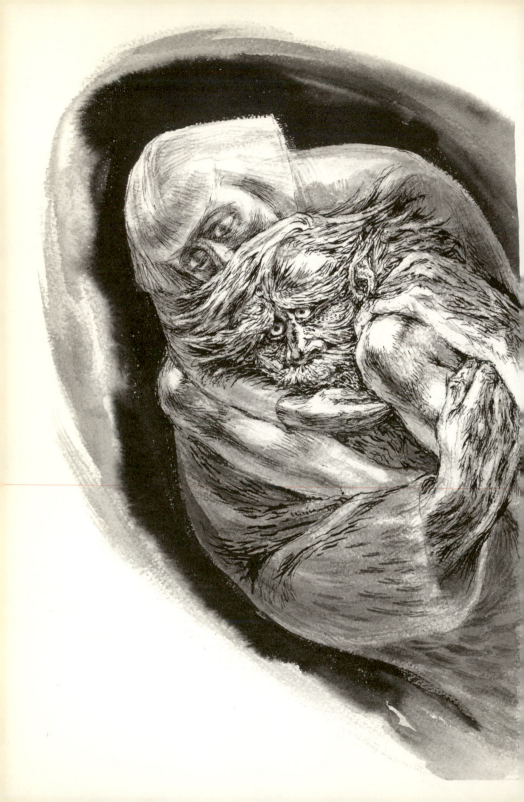

and at the bottom lay
a wild man,
his body rusty brown.
His hair covering his knees.
Perhaps he was no more dangerous
than a hummingbird;
perhaps he was Christ's boy-child;
perhaps he was only bruised like an apple
but he appeared to them to be a lunatic.
The king placed him in a large iron cage
in the courtyard of his palace.
The court gathered around the wild man
and munched peanuts and sold balloons
and not until he cried out:
Agony! Agony!
did they move off.

The king's son
was playing with his ball one day
and it rolled into the iron cage.
It appeared as suddenly as a gallstone.
The wild man did not complain.
He talked calmly to the boy
and convinced him to unlock the cage.
The wild man carried him and his ball
piggyback off into the woods
promising him good luck and gold for life.

The wild man set the boy at a golden spring
and asked him to guard it from a fox

or a feather that might pollute it.
The boy agreed and took up residence there.
The first night he dipped his finger in.
It turned to gold; as gold as a fountain pen,
but the wild man forgave him.
The second night he bent to take a drink
and his hair got wet, turning as gold
as Midas' daughter.
As stiff as the Medusa hair of a Greek statue.
This time the wild man could not forgive him.
He sent the boy out into the world.
But if you have great need, he said,
you may come into the forest and call *Iron Hans*
and I will come to help you for you
were the only one who was kind
to this accursed bull of a wild man.

The boy went out into the world,
his gold hair tucked under a cap.
He found work as a gardener's boy
at a far-off castle. All day set out
under the red ball to dig and weed.
One day he picked some wildflowers
for the princess and took them to her.
She demanded he take off his cap
in her presence. You look like a jester,
she taunted him, but he would not.
You look like a bird, she taunted him,
and snatched off the cap.
His hair fell down with a clang.

It fell down like a moon chain
and it delighted her.
The princess fell in love.

Next there was a war
that the king was due to lose.
The boy went into the forest
and called out: Iron Hans, Iron Hans,
and the wild man appeared.
He gave the boy a black charger,
a sword as sharp as a guillotine
and a great body of black knights.
They went forth and cut the enemy down
like a row of cabbage heads.
Then they vanished.
The court talked of nothing
but the unknown knight in a cap.
The princess thought of the boy
but the head gardener said:
Not he. He had only a three-legged horse.
He could have done better with a stork.
Three days in a row,
the princess, hoping to lure him back,
threw a gold ball.
Remember back,
the boy was good at losing balls
but was he good at catching them?
Three days running the boy,
thanks to Iron Hans,
performed like Joe Dimaggio.

And thus they were married.

At the wedding feast
the music stopped suddenly
and a door flew open
and a proud king walked in
and embraced the boy.
Of course
it was Iron Hans.
He had been bewitched
and the boy had broken the spell.
He who slays the warrior
and captures the maiden's heart
undoes the spell.
He who kills his father
and thrice wins his mother
undoes the spell.

Without Thorazine
or benefit of psychotherapy
Iron Hans was transformed.
No need for Master Medical;
no need for electroshock —
merely bewitched all along.
Just as the frog who was a prince.
Just as the madman his simple boyhood.

When I was a wild man,
Iron Hans said,
I tarnished all the world.

I was the infector.
I was the poison breather.
I was a professional,
but you have saved me
from the awful babble
of that calling.

CINDERELLA

You always read about it:
the plumber with twelve children
who wins the Irish Sweepstakes.
From toilets to riches.
That story.

Or the nursemaid,
some luscious sweet from Denmark
who captures the oldest son's heart.
From diapers to Dior.
That story.

Or a milkman who serves the wealthy,
eggs, cream, butter, yogurt, milk,
the white truck like an ambulance
who goes into real estate
and makes a pile.
From homogenized to martinis at lunch.

Or the charwoman
who is on the bus when it cracks up
and collects enough from the insurance.

From mops to Bonwit Teller.
That story.

Once
the wife of a rich man was on her deathbed
and she said to her daughter Cinderella:
Be devout. Be good. Then I will smile
down from heaven in the seam of a cloud.
The man took another wife who had
two daughters, pretty enough
but with hearts like blackjacks.
Cinderella was their maid.
She slept on the sooty hearth each night
and walked around looking like Al Jolson.
Her father brought presents home from town,
jewels and gowns for the other women
but the twig of a tree for Cinderella.
She planted that twig on her mother's grave
and it grew to a tree where a white dove sat.
Whenever she wished for anything the dove
would drop it like an egg upon the ground.
The bird is important, my dears, so heed him.

Next came the ball, as you all know.
It was a marriage market.
The prince was looking for a wife.
All but Cinderella were preparing
and gussying up for the big event.
Cinderella begged to go too.
Her stepmother threw a dish of lentils

into the cinders and said: Pick them
up in an hour and you shall go.
The white dove brought all his friends;
all the warm wings of the fatherland came,
and picked up the lentils in a jiffy.
No, Cinderella, said the stepmother,
you have no clothes and cannot dance.
That's the way with stepmothers.

Cinderella went to the tree at the grave
and cried forth like a gospel singer:
Mama! Mama! My turtledove,
send me to the prince's ball!
The bird dropped down a golden dress
and delicate little gold slippers.
Rather a large package for a simple bird.
So she went. Which is no surprise.
Her stepmother and sisters didn't
recognize her without her cinder face
and the prince took her hand on the spot
and danced with no other the whole day.

As nightfall came she thought she'd better
get home. The prince walked her home
and she disappeared into the pigeon house
and although the prince took an axe and broke
it open she was gone. Back to her cinders.
These events repeated themselves for three days.
However on the third day the prince
covered the palace steps with cobbler's wax
and Cinderella's gold shoe stuck upon it.

Now he would find whom the shoe fit
and find his strange dancing girl for keeps.
He went to their house and the two sisters
were delighted because they had lovely feet.
The eldest went into a room to try the slipper on
but her big toe got in the way so she simply
sliced it off and put on the slipper.
The prince rode away with her until the white dove
told him to look at the blood pouring forth.
That is the way with amputations.
They don't just heal up like a wish.
The other sister cut off her heel
but the blood told as blood will.
The prince was getting tired.
He began to feel like a shoe salesman.
But he gave it one last try.
This time Cinderella fit into the shoe
like a love letter into its envelope.

At the wedding ceremony
the two sisters came to curry favor
and the white dove pecked their eyes out.
Two hollow spots were left
like soup spoons.

Cinderella and the prince
lived, they say, happily ever after,
like two dolls in a museum case
never bother by diapers or dust,
never arguing over the timing of an egg,

never telling the same story twice,
never getting a middle-aged spread,
their darling smiles pasted on for eternity.
Regular Bobbsey Twins.
That story.

ONE-EYE, TWO-EYES,
THREE-EYES

Even in the pink crib
the somehow deficient,
the somehow maimed,
are thought to have
a special pipeline to the mystical,
the faint smell of the occult,
a large ear on the God-horn.

Still,
the parents have bizarre thoughts,
thoughts like a skill saw.
They accuse: Your grandfather,
your bad sperm, your evil ovary.
Thinking: The devil has put his finger upon us.
And yet in time
they consult their astrologer
and admire their trophy.
They turn a radish into a ruby.
They plan an elaborate celebration.
They warm to their roles.
They carry it off with a positive fervor.

The bird who cannot fly
is left like a cockroach.
A three-legged kitten is carried
by the scruff of the neck
and dropped into a blind cellar hole.
A malformed foal would not be nursed.
Nature takes care of nature.

I knew a child once
With the mind of a hen.
She was the favored one
for she was as innocent as a snowflake
and was a great lover of music.
She could have been a candidate
for the International Bach Society
but she was only a primitive.
A harmonica would do.
Love grew around her like crabgrass.
Even though she might live to the age of fifty
her mother planned a Mass of the Angels
and wore her martyrdom
like a string of pearls.

The unusual needs to be commented upon . . .
The Thalidomide babies
with flippers at their shoulders,
wearing their mechanical arms
like derricks.
The club-footed boy
wearing his shoe like a flat iron.

The idiot child,
a stuffed doll who can only masturbate.
The hunchback carrying his hump
like a bag of onions . . .
Oh how we treasure
their scenic value.

When a child stays needy until he is fifty —
oh mother-eye, oh mother-eye, crush me in —
the parent is as strong as a telephone pole.

Once upon a time
there were three sisters.
One with one eye
like a great blue aggie.
One with two eyes,
common as pennies.
One with three eyes,
the third like an intern.
Their mother loved only One-Eye and Three.
She loved them because they were God's lie.
And she liked to poke
at the unusual holes in their faces.
Two-Eyes was as ordinary
as an old man with a big belly
and she despised her.
Two-Eyes wore only rags
and ate only scraps from the dog's dish
and spent her days caring for their goat.

One day,
off in the fields with the goat
Two-Eyes cried, her cheeks as wet as a trout
and an old woman appeared before her
and promised if she sang to her goat
a feast would always be provided.
Two-Eyes sang and there appeared a table
as rich as one at Le Pavillon
and each dish bloomed like floribunda.
Two-Eyes, her eyes as matched as a pen and pencil set,
ate all she could.
This went on in a secret manner
until the mother and sisters saw
that she was not lapping from the dog dish.
So One-Eye came with her and her goat
to see where and how she got the secret food.
However Two-Eyes sang to her as softly as milk
and soon she fell fast asleep.
In this way Two-Eyes enjoyed her usual magic meal.
Next the mother sent Three-Eyes to watch.
Again Two-Eyes sang and again her sister fell asleep.
However her third eye did not shut.
It stayed as open as a clam on a half shell
and thus she witnessed the magic meal,
thus the mother heard all of it
and thus they killed the goat.

Again Two-Eyes cried like a trout
and again the old woman came to her
and told her to take some of the insides
of the slaughtered goat and bury them
in front of the cottage.
She carried forth the green and glossy intestine
and buried it where she was told.
The next morning they all saw
a great tree with leaves of silver
glittering like tinfoil
and apples made of fourteen carat gold.
One-Eye tried to climb up and pick one
but the branches merely withdrew.
Three-Eyes tried and the branches withdrew.
The mother tried and the branches withdrew.
May I try, said Two-Eyes,
but they replied:
You with your two eyes,
what can you do?
Yet when she climbed up and reached out
an apple came into her hand
as simply as a chicken laying her daily egg.

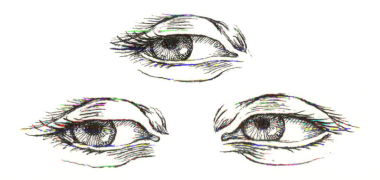

They bade her come down from the tree to hide
as a handsome knight was riding their way.
He stopped
and admired the tree
as you knew he would.
They claimed the tree as theirs
and he said sadly:
He who owns a branch of that tree
would have all he wished for in this world.
The two sisters clipped around the tree
like a pair of miming clowns
but not a branch or an apple came their way.
The tree treated them like poison ivy.
At last Two-Eyes came forth
and easily broke off a branch for him.

Quite naturally the knight carried her off
and the sisters were overjoyed
as now the tree would belong to them.
It burned in their brains like radium
but the next morning the tree had vanished.
The tree had, in the way of such magic,
followed Two-Eyes to the castle.
The knight married her
and she wore gowns as lovely as kisses
and ate goose liver and peaches
whenever she wished.

Years later
two beggars came to the castle,

along with the fishermen and the peasants
and the whole mournful lot.
These beggars were none other than her sisters
wearing their special eyes,
one the Cyclops,
one the pawnshop.
Two-Eyes was kind to them
and took them in
for they were magical.
They were to become her Stonehenge,
her cosmic investment,
her seals, her rings, her urns
and she became as strong as Moses.
Two-Eyes was kind to them
and took them in
because they were needy.
They were to become her children,
her charmed cripples, her hybrids —
oh mother-eye, oh mother-eye, crush me in.
So they took root in her heart
with their religious hunger.

THE WONDERFUL MUSICIAN

My sisters,
do you remember the fiddlers
of your youth?
Those dances
so like a drunkard
lighting a fire in the belly?
That speech,
as piercing as a loon's,
exciting both mayors
and cab drivers?
Sometimes,
ear to the bedside radio,
frozen on your cot
like a humped hairpin,
or jolt upright in the wind
on alternating current
like a fish on the hook
dancing the death dance,
remember
the vibrato,
a wasp in the ear?
Remember dancing in

those electric shoes?
Remember?
Remember music
and beware.

Consider
the wonderful musician
who goes quite alone
through the forest
and plays his fiddle-me-roo
to bring forth a companion.
The fox
was a womanly sort,
his tongue lapping a mirror.
But when he heard the music
he danced forth
in those electric shoes
and promised his life
if he too could learn to play.
The musician despised the fox
but nevertheless he said,
You have only to do as I bid you.
The fox replied,
I will obey you as
a scholar obeys his master.
Thus the musician
took him to an oak tree
and bade him put his left paw
in its wooden slit.
Then he fixed him with a wedge

until he was caught.
The fox was left there
kneeling like Romeo.

The musician went on
playing his fiddle-me-roo
to bring forth a companion.
The wolf,
a greedy creature,
his eye on the soup kettle,
heard the music
and danced forth
in those electric shoes.
He came forth
and was bilked
by the same order.
The musician fastened
both his paws to a hazel bush
and he hung spread-eagle
on a miniature crucifix.

The musician went on
playing his fiddle-me-roo
to bring forth a companion.
The hare,
a child of the dark,
his tail twitching
over the cellar hole,
came forth and was had.
With a rope around his throat

he ran twenty times around the maypole
until he foamed up
like a rabid dog.

The fox
as clever as a martyr
freed himself
and coming upon the crucifixion
and the rabid dog,
undid them
and all three swept
through the forest
to tear off the musician's
ten wonderful fingers.

The musician had gone on
playing his fiddle-me-roo.
Old kiteskin,
the bird,
had seen the persecution
and lay as still
as a dollar bill.
Old drowse-belly,
the snake,
did not come forth —
He lay as still as a ruler.
But a poor woodcutter
came forth with his axe
promising his life
for that music.

The wolf, the fox,
and the hare
came in for the kill.
The woodcutter
held up his axe —
it glinted like a steak knife —
and forecast their death.
They scuttled back into the wood
and the musician played
fiddle-me-roo
once more.
Saved by his gift
like many of us —
little Eichmanns,
little mothers —
I'd say.

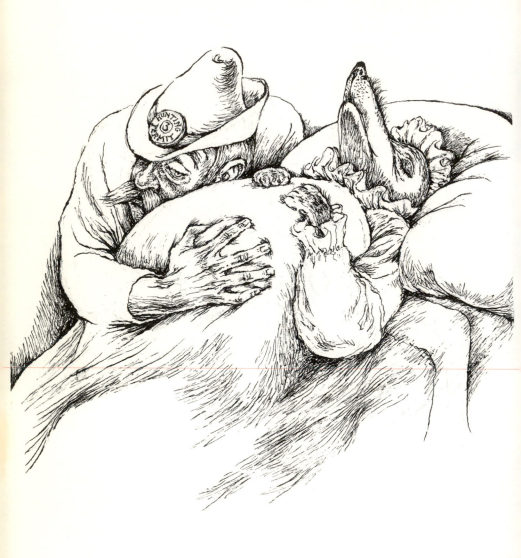

RED RIDING HOOD

Many are the deceivers:

The suburban matron,
proper in the supermarket,
list in hand so she won't suddenly fly,
buying her Duz and Chuck Wagon dog food,
meanwhile ascending from earth,
letting her stomach fill up with helium,
letting her arms go loose as kite tails,
getting ready to meet her lover
a mile down Apple Crest Road
in the Congregational Church parking lot.

Two seemingly respectable women
come up to an old Jenny
and show her an envelope
full of money
and promise to share the booty
if she'll give them ten thou
as an act of faith.
Her life savings are under the mattress
covered with rust stains

and counting.
They are as wrinkled as prunes
but negotiable.
The two women take the money and disappear.
Where is the moral?
Not all knives are for
stabbing the exposed belly.
Rock climbs on rock
and it only makes a seashore.
Old Jenny has lost her belief in mattresses
and now she has no wastebasket in which
to keep her youth.

The standup comic
on the "Tonight" show
who imitates the Vice President
and cracks up Johnny Carson
and delays sleep for millions
of bedfellows watching between their feet,
slits his wrist the next morning
in the Algonquin's old-fashioned bathroom,
the razor in his hand like a toothbrush,
wall as anonymous as a urinal,
the shower curtain his slack rubberman audience,
and then the slash
as simple as opening a letter
and the warm blood breaking out like a rose
upon the bathtub with its claw and ball feet.

And I. I too.
Quite collected at cocktail parties,

meanwhile in my head
I'm undergoing open-heart surgery.
The heart, poor fellow,
pounding on his little tin drum
with a faint death beat.
The heart, that eyeless beetle,
enormous that Kafka beetle,
running panicked through his maze,
never stopping one foot after the other
one hour after the other
until he gags on an apple
and it's all over.

And I. I too again.
I built a summer house on Cape Ann.
A simple A-frame and this too was
a deception — nothing haunts a new house.
When I moved in with a bathing suit and tea bags
the ocean rumbled like a train backing up
and at each window secrets came in
like gas. My mother, that departed soul,
sat in my Eames chair and reproached me
for losing her keys to the old cottage.
Even in the electric kitchen there was
the smell of a journey. The ocean
was seeping through its frontiers
and laying me out on its wet rails.
The bed was stale with my childhood
and I could not move to another city
where the worthy make a new life.

Long ago
there was a strange deception:
a wolf dressed in frills,
a kind of transvestite.
But I get ahead of my story.
In the beginning
there was just little Red Riding Hood,
so called because her grandmother
made her a red cape and she was never without it.
It was her Linus blanket, besides
it was red, as red as the Swiss flag,
yes it was red, as red as chicken blood.
But more than she loved her riding hood
she loved her grandmother who lived
far from the city in the big wood.

This one day her mother gave her
a basket of wine and cake
to take to her grandmother
because she was ill.
Wine and cake?
Where's the aspirin? The penicillin?
Where's the fruit juice?
Peter Rabbit got camomile tea.
But wine and cake it was.

On her way in the big wood
Red Riding Hood met the wolf.
Good day, Mr. Wolf, she said,
thinking him no more dangerous

than a streetcar or a panhandler.
He asked where she was going
and she obligingly told him.
There among the roots and trunks
with the mushrooms pulsing inside the moss
he planned how to eat them both,
the grandmother an old carrot
and the child a shy budkin
in a red red hood.
He bade her to look at the bloodroot,
the small bunchberry and the dogtooth
and pick some for her grandmother.
And this she did.
Meanwhile he scampered off
to Grandmother's house and ate her up
as quick as a slap.
Then he put on her nightdress and cap
and snuggled down into the bed.
A deceptive fellow.

Red Riding Hood
knocked on the door and entered
with her flowers, her cake, her wine.
Grandmother looked strange,
a dark and hairy disease it seemed.
Oh Grandmother, what big ears you have,
ears, eyes, hands and then the teeth.
The better to eat you with, my dear.
So the wolf gobbled Red Riding Hood down
like a gumdrop. Now he was fat.

He appeared to be in his ninth month
and Red Riding Hood and her grandmother
rode like two Jonahs up and down with
his every breath. One pigeon. One partridge.

He was fast asleep,
dreaming in his cap and gown,
wolfless.
Along came a huntsman who heard
the loud contented snores
and knew that was no grandmother.
He opened the door and said,
So it's you, old sinner.
He raised his gun to shoot him
when it occurred to him that maybe
the wolf had eaten up the old lady.
So he took a knife and began cutting open
the sleeping wolf, a kind of caesarian section.

It was a carnal knife that let
Red Riding Hood out like a poppy,
quite alive from the kingdom of the belly.
And grandmother too
still waiting for cakes and wine.
The wolf, they decided, was too mean
to be simply shot so they filled his belly
with large stones and sewed him up.
He was as heavy as a cemetery
and when he woke up and tried to run off
he fell over dead. Killed by his own weight.
Many a deception ends on such a note.

The huntsman and the grandmother and Red Riding
    Hood
sat down by his corpse and had a meal of wine and
    cake.
Those two remembering
nothing naked and brutal
from that little death,
that little birth,
from their going down
and their lifting up.

THE MAIDEN
WITHOUT HANDS

Is it possible
he marries a cripple
out of admiration?
A desire to own the maiming
so that not one of us butchers
will come to him with crowbars
or slim precise tweezers?
Lady, bring me your wooden leg
so I may stand on my own
two pink pig feet.
If someone burns out your eye
I will take your socket
and use it for an ashtray.
If they have cut out your uterus
I will give you a laurel wreath
to put in its place.
If you have cut off your ear
I will give you a crow
who will hear just as well.
My apple has no worm in it!
My apple is whole!

Once
there was a cruel father
who cut off his daughter's hands
to escape from the wizard.
The maiden held up her stumps
as helpless as dog's paws
and that made the wizard
want her. He wanted to lap
her up like strawberry preserve.
She cried on her stumps
as sweet as lotus water,
as strong as petroleum,
as sure-fire as castor oil.
Her tears lay around her like a moat.
Her tears so purified her
that the wizard could not approach.

She left her father's house
to wander in forbidden woods,
the good, kind king's woods.
She stretched her neck like an elastic,
up, up, to take a bite of a pear
hanging from the king's tree.
Picture her there for a moment,
a perfect still life.
After all,
she could not feed herself
or pull her pants down
or brush her teeth.

She was, I'd say,

without resources.
The king spied upon her at
that moment of stretching up, up
and he thought,
Eeny, Meeny, Miny, Mo —
There but for the grace of —
I will take her for my wife.

And thus they were married
and lived together on a sugar cube.
The king had silver hands made for her.
They were polished daily and kept in place,
little tin mittens.
The court bowed at the sight of them from a distance.
The leisurely passerby stopped and crossed himself.
What a fellow he is, they said of the king,
and kept their lips pursed as for a kiss.
But that was not the last word
for the king was called to war.
Naturally the queen was pregnant
so the king left her in care of his mother.
Buy her a perambulator, he said,
and send me a message when my son is born.
Let me hear no catcalls
or see a burned mattress.
He was superstitious.
You can see his point of view.

When the son was born
the mother sent a message

but the wizard intercepted it,
saying, instead, a changeling was born.
The king didn't mind.
He was used to this sort of thing by now.
He said: Take care,
but the wizard intercepted it,
saying: Kill both;
then cut out her eyes and send them,
also cut out his tongue and send it;
I will want my proof.

The mother,
now the grandmother —
a strange vocation to be a mother at all —
told them to run off in the woods.
The queen named her son
Painbringer
and fled to a safe cottage in the woods.
She and Painbringer were so good in the woods
that her hands grew back.
The ten fingers budding like asparagus,
the palms as whole as pancakes,
as soft and pink as face powder.

The king returned to the castle
and heard the news from his mother
and then he set out for seven years in the woods
never once eating a thing,
or so he said,
doing far better than Mahatma Gandhi.

He was good and kind as I have already said
so he found his beloved.
She brought forth the silver hands.
She brought forth Painbringer
and he realized they were his,
though both now unfortunately whole.
Now the butchers will come to *me*,
he thought, for I have lost my luck.
It put an insidious fear in him
like a tongue depressor held fast
at the back of your throat.
But he was good and kind
so he made the best of it
like a switch hitter.

They returned to the castle
and had a second wedding feast.
He put a ring on her finger this time
and they danced like dandies.
All their lives they kept the silver hands,
polished daily,
a kind of purple heart,
a talisman,
a yellow star.

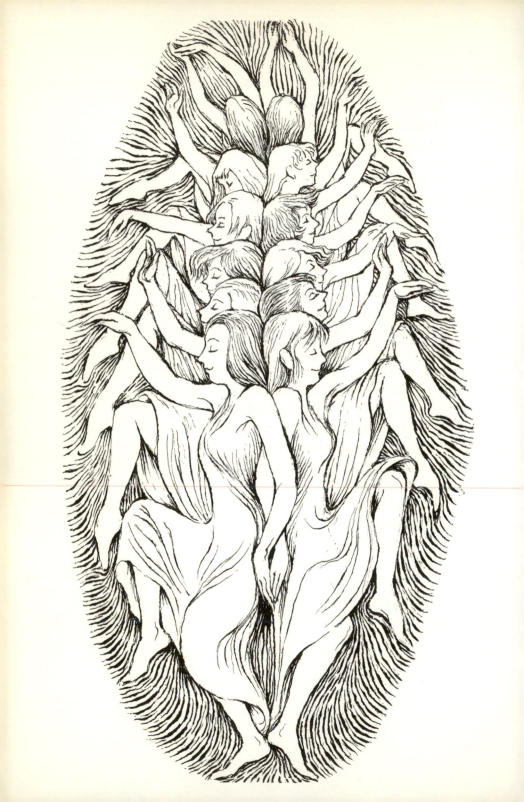

THE TWELVE DANCING
PRINCESSES

If you danced from midnight
to six A.M. who would understand?

The runaway boy
who chucks it all
to live on the Boston Common
on speed and saltines,
pissing in the duck pond,
rapping with the street priest,
trading talk like blows,
another missing person,
would understand.

The paralytic's wife
who takes her love to town,
sitting on the bar stool,
downing stingers and peanuts,
singing "That ole Ace down in the hole,"
would understand.

The passengers
from Boston to Paris

87

watching the movie with dawn
coming up like statues of honey,
having partaken of champagne and steak
while the world turned like a toy globe,
those murderers of the nightgown
would understand.

The amnesiac
who tunes into a new neighborhood,
having misplaced the past,
having thrown out someone else's
credit cards and monogrammed watch,
would understand.

The drunken poet
(a genius by daylight)
who places long-distance calls
at three A.M. and then lets you sit
holding the phone while he vomits
(he calls it "The Night of the Long Knives")
getting his kicks out of the death call,
would understand.

The insomniac
listening to his heart
thumping like a June bug,
listening on his transistor
to Long John Nebel arguing from New York,
lying on his bed like a stone table,
would understand.

The night nurse
with her eyes slit like Venetian blinds,
she of the tubes and the plasma,
listening to the heart monitor,
the death cricket bleeping,
she who calls you "we"
and keeps vigil like a ballistic missile,
would understand.

Once
this king had twelve daughters,
each more beautiful than the other.
They slept together, bed by bed
in a kind of girls' dormitory.
At night the king locked and bolted the door.
How could they possibly escape?
Yet each morning their shoes
were danced to pieces.
Each was as worn as an old jockstrap.
The king sent out a proclamation
that anyone who could discover
where the princesses did their dancing
could take his pick of the litter.
However there was a catch.
If he failed, he would pay with his life.
Well, so it goes.

Many princes tried,
each sitting outside the dormitory,
the door ajar so he could observe

89

what enchantment came over the shoes.
But each time the twelve dancing princesses
gave the snoopy man a Mickey Finn
and so he was beheaded.
Poof! Like a basketball.

It so happened that a poor soldier
heard about these strange goings on
and decided to give it a try.
On his way to the castle
he met an old old woman.
Age, for a change, was of some use.
She wasn't stuffed in a nursing home.
She told him not to drink a drop of wine
and gave him a cloak that would make
him invisible when the right time came.
And thus he sat outside the dorm.
The oldest princess brought him some wine
but he fastened a sponge beneath his chin,
looking the opposite of Andy Gump.

The sponge soaked up the wine,
and thus he stayed awake.
He feigned sleep however
and the princesses sprang out of their beds
and fussed around like a Miss America Contest.
Then the eldest went to her bed
and knocked upon it and it sank into the earth.
They descended down the opening
one after the other. The crafty soldier

put on his invisible cloak and followed.
Yikes, said the youngest daughter,
something just stepped on my dress.
But the oldest thought it just a nail.

Next stood an avenue of trees,
each leaf made of sterling silver.
The soldier took a leaf for proof.
The youngest heard the branch break
and said, Oof! Who goes there?
But the oldest said, Those are
the royal trumpets playing triumphantly.
The next trees were made of diamonds.
He took one that flickered like Tinkerbell
and the youngest said: Wait up! He is here!
But the oldest said: Trumpets, my dear.

Next they came to a lake where lay
twelve boats with twelve enchanted princes
waiting to row them to the underground castle.
The soldier sat in the youngest's boat
and the boat was as heavy as if an icebox
had been added but the prince did not suspect.

Next came the ball where the shoes did duty.
The princesses danced like taxi girls at Roseland
as if those tickets would run right out.
They were painted in kisses with their secret hair
and though the soldier drank from their cups
they drank down their youth with nary a thought.

Cruets of champagne and cups full of rubies.
They danced until morning and the sun came up
naked and angry and so they returned
by the same strange route. The soldier
went forward through the dormitory and into
his waiting chair to feign his druggy sleep.
That morning the soldier, his eyes fiery
like blood in a wound, his purpose brutal
as if facing a battle, hurried with his answer
as if to the Sphinx. The shoes! The shoes!
The soldier told. He brought forth
the silver leaf, the diamond the size of a plum.

He had won. The dancing shoes would dance
no more. The princesses were torn from
their night life like a baby from its pacifier.
Because he was old he picked the eldest.
At the wedding the princesses averted their eyes
and sagged like old sweatshirts.
Now the runaways would run no more and never
again would their hair be tangled into diamonds,
never again their shoes worn down to a laugh,
never the bed falling down into purgatory
to let them climb in after
with their Lucifer kicking.

THE FROG PRINCE

Frau Doktor,
Mama Brundig,
take out your contacts,
remove your wig.

I write for you.
I entertain.
But frogs come out
of the sky like rain.

Frogs arrive
With an ugly fury.
You are my judge.
You are my jury.

My guilts are what
we catalogue.
I'll take a knife
and chop up frog.

Frog has no nerves.
Frog is as old as a cockroach.

Frog is my father's genitals.
Frog is a malformed doorknob.
Frog is a soft bag of green.

The moon will not have him.
The sun wants to shut off
like a light bulb.
At the sight of him
the stone washes itself in a tub.
The crow thinks he's an apple
and drops a worm in.
At the feel of frog
the touch-me-nots explode
like electric slugs.

Slime will have him.
Slime has made him a house.

Mr. Poison
is at my bed.
He wants my sausage.
He wants my bread.

Mama Brundig,
he wants my beer.
He wants my Christ
for a souvenir.

Frog has boil disease
and a bellyful of parasites.

He says: Kiss me. Kiss me.
And the ground soils itself.

Why
should a certain
quite adorable princess
be walking in her garden
at such a time
and toss her golden ball
up like a bubble
and drop it into the well?
It was ordained.
Just as the fates deal out
the plague with a tarot card.
Just as the Supreme Being drills
holes in our skulls to let
the Boston Symphony through.

But I digress.
A loss has taken place.
The ball has sunk like a cast-iron pot
into the bottom of the well.

Lost, she said,
my moon, my butter calf,
my yellow moth, my Hindu hare.
Obviously it was more than a ball.
Balls such as these are not
for sale in Au Bon Marché.
I took the moon, she said,

between my teeth
and now it is gone
and I am lost forever.
A thief had robbed by day.

Suddenly the well grew
thick and boiling
and a frog appeared.
His eyes bulged like two peas
and his body was trussed into place.
Do not be afraid, Princess,
he said, I am not a vagabond,
a cattle farmer, a shepherd,
a doorkeeper, a postman
or a laborer.
I come to you as a tradesman.
I have something to sell.
Your ball, he said,
for just three things.
Let me eat from your plate.
Let me drink from your cup.
Let me sleep in your bed.
She thought, Old Waddler,
those three you will never do,
but she made the promises
with hopes for her ball once more.
He brought it up in his mouth
like a tricky old dog
and she ran back to the castle
leaving the frog quite alone.

That evening at dinner time
a knock was heard at the castle door
and a voice demanded:
King's youngest daughter,
let me in. You promised;
now open to me.
I have left the skunk cabbage
and the eels to live with you.
The king then heard of her promise
and forced her to comply.
The frog first sat on her lap.
He was as awful as an undertaker.
Next he was at her plate
looking over her bacon
and calves' liver.

We will eat in tandem,
he said gleefully.
Her fork trembled
as if a small machine
had entered her.
He sat upon the liver
and partook like a gourmet.
The princess choked
as if she were eating a puppy.
From her cup he drank.
It wasn't exactly hygienic.
From her cup she drank
as if it were Socrates' hemlock.

Next came the bed.
The silky royal bed.
Ah! The penultimate hour!
There was the pillow
with the princess breathing
and there was the sinuous frog
riding up and down beside her.
I have been lost in a river
of shut doors, he said,
and I have made my way over
the wet stones to live with you.
She woke up aghast.
I suffer for birds and fireflies
but not frogs, she said,
and threw him across the room.
Kaboom!

Like a genie coming out of a samovar,
a handsome prince arose in the
corner of her royal bedroom.
He had kind eyes and hands
and was a friend of sorrow.
Thus they were married.
After all he had compromised her.

He hired a night watchman
so that no one could enter the chamber
and he had the well
boarded over so that
never again would she lose her ball,
that moon, that Krishna hair,
that blind poppy, that innocent globe,
that madonna womb.

HANSEL AND GRETEL

Little plum,
said the mother to her son,
I want to bite,
I want to chew,
I will eat you up.
Little child,
little nubkin,
sweet as fudge,
you are my blitz.
I will spit on you for luck
for you are better than money.
Your neck as smooth
as a hard-boiled egg;
soft cheeks, my pears,
let me buzz you on the neck
and take a bite.
I have a pan that will fit you.
Just pull up your knees like a game hen.
Let me take your pulse
and set the oven for 350.
Come, my pretender, my fritter,
my bubbler, my chicken biddy!

Oh succulent one,
it is but one turn in the road
and I would be a cannibal!

Hansel and Gretel
and their parents
had come upon evil times.
They had cooked the dog
and served him up like lamb chops.
There was only a loaf of bread left.
The final solution,
their mother told their father,
was to lose the children in the forest.
We have enough bread for ourselves
but none for them.
Hansel heard this
and took pebbles with him
into the forest.
He dropped a pebble every fifth step
and later, after their parents had left them,
they followed the pebbles home.
The next day their mother gave them
each a hunk of bread
like a page out of the Bible
and sent them out again.
This time Hansel dropped bits of bread.
The birds, however, ate the bread
and they were lost at last.
They were blind as worms.
They turned like ants in a glove

not knowing which direction to take.
The sun was in Leo
and water spouted from the lion's head
but still they did not know their way.

So they walked for twenty days
and twenty nights
and came upon a rococo house
made all of food from its windows
to its chocolate chimney.
A witch lived in that house
and she took them in.
She gave them a large supper
to fatten them up
and then they slept,
z's buzzing from their mouths like flies.
Then she took Hansel,
the smarter, the bigger,
the juicier, into the barn
and locked him up.
Each day she fed him goose liver
so that he would fatten,
so that he would be as larded
as a plump coachman,
that knight of the whip.
She was planning to cook him
and then gobble him up
as in a feast
after a holy war.

She spoke to Gretel

and told her how her brother
would be better than mutton;
how a thrill would go through her
as she smelled him cooking;
how she would lay the table
and sharpen the knives
and neglect none of the refinements.
Gretel
who had said nothing so far
nodded her head and wept.
She who neither dropped pebbles or bread
bided her time.

The witch looked upon her
with new eyes and thought:
Why not this saucy lass
for an hors d'oeuvre?
She explained to Gretel
that she must climb into the oven
to see if she would fit.
Gretel spoke at last:
Ja, Fräulein, show me how it can be done.
The witch thought this fair
and climbed in to show the way.
It was a matter of gymnastics.
Gretel,
seeing her moment in history,
shut fast the oven,
locked fast the door,
fast as Houdini,

and turned the oven on to bake.
The witch turned as red
as the Jap flag.
Her blood began to boil up
like Coca-Cola.
Her eyes began to melt.
She was done for.
Altogether a memorable incident.

As for Hansel and Gretel,
they escaped and went home to their father.
Their mother,
you'll be glad to hear, was dead.
Only at suppertime
while eating a chicken leg
did our children remember
the woe of the oven,
the smell of the cooking witch,
a little like mutton,
to be served only with burgundy
and fine white linen
like something religious.

BRIAR ROSE
(SLEEPING BEAUTY)

Consider
a girl who keeps slipping off,
arms limp as old carrots,
into the hypnotist's trance,
into a spirit world
speaking with the gift of tongues.
She is stuck in the time machine,
suddenly two years old sucking her thumb,
as inward as a snail,
learning to talk again.
She's on a voyage.
She is swimming further and further back,
up like a salmon,
struggling into her mother's pocketbook.
Little doll child,
come here to Papa.
Sit on my knee.
I have kisses for the back of your neck.
A penny for your thoughts, Princess.
I will hunt them like an emerald.
Come be my snooky
and I will give you a root.

That kind of voyage,
rank as honeysuckle.

Once
a king had a christening
for his daughter Briar Rose
and because he had only twelve gold plates
he asked only twelve fairies
to the grand event.
The thirteenth fairy,
her fingers as long and thin as straws,
her eyes burnt by cigarettes,
her uterus an empty teacup,
arrived with an evil gift.
She made this prophecy:
The princess shall prick herself
on a spinning wheel in her fifteenth year
and then fall down dead.
Kaputt!
The court fell silent.
The king looked like Munch's *Scream*.
Fairies' prophecies,
in times like those,
held water.
However the twelfth fairy
had a certain kind of eraser
and thus she mitigated the curse
changing that death
into a hundred-year sleep.

The king ordered every spinning wheel
exterminated and exorcized.
Briar Rose grew to be a goddess
and each night the king
bit the hem of her gown
to keep her safe.
He fastened the moon up
with a safety pin
to give her perpetual light
He forced every male in the court
to scour his tongue with Bab-o
lest they poison the air she dwelt in.
Thus she dwelt in his odor.
Rank as honeysuckle.

On her fifteenth birthday
she pricked her finger
on a charred spinning wheel
and the clocks stopped.
Yes indeed. She went to sleep.
The king and queen went to sleep,
the courtiers, the flies on the wall.
The fire in the hearth grew still
and the roast meat stopped crackling.
The trees turned into metal
and the dog became china.
They all lay in a trance,
each a catatonic
stuck in the time machine.
Even the frogs were zombies.

Only a bunch of briar roses grew
forming a great wall of tacks
around the castle.
Many princes
tried to get through the brambles
for they had heard much of Briar Rose
but they had not scoured their tongues
so they were held by the thorns
and thus were crucified.
In due time
a hundred years passed
and a prince got through.
The briars parted as if for Moses
and the prince found the tableau intact.
He kissed Briar Rose
and she woke up crying:
Daddy! Daddy!
Presto! She's out of prison!
She married the prince
and all went well
except for the fear —
the fear of sleep.

Briar Rose
was an insomniac . . .
She could not nap
or lie in sleep
without the court chemist
mixing her some knock-out drops
and never in the prince's presence.

If it is to come, she said,
sleep must take me unawares
while I am laughing or dancing
so that I do not know that brutal place
where I lie down with cattle prods,
the hole in my cheek open.
Further, I must not dream
for when I do I see the table set
and a faltering crone at my place,
her eyes burnt by cigarettes
as she eats betrayal like a slice of meat.

I must not sleep
for while asleep I'm ninety
and think I'm dying.
Death rattles in my throat
like a marble.
I wear tubes like earrings.
I lie as still as a bar of iron.
You can stick a needle
through my kneecap and I won't flinch.
I'm all shot up with Novocain.
This trance girl
is yours to do with.
You could lay her in a grave,
an awful package,
and shovel dirt on her face
and she'd never call back: Hello there!
But if you kissed her on the mouth
her eyes would spring open

and she'd call out: Daddy! Daddy!
Presto!
She's out of prison.

There was a theft.
That much I am told.
I was abandoned.
That much I know.
I was forced backward.
I was forced forward.
I was passed hand to hand
like a bowl of fruit.
Each night I am nailed into place
and I forget who I am.
Daddy?
That's another kind of prison.
It's not the prince at all,
but my father
drunkenly bent over my bed,
circling the abyss like a shark,
my father thick upon me
like some sleeping jellyfish.

What voyage this, little girl?
This coming out of prison?
God help —
this life after death?

Anne Sexton was born in Newton, Massachusetts. She grew up in Wellesley and now lives in Weston with her husband and two daughters. Her first book, *To Bedlam and Part Way Back* (1960), and her second, *All My Pretty Ones* (1962), early established her as one of our outstanding American poets. *Live or Die* (1966) won her the Pulitzer Prize for Poetry. Her *Love Poems* appeared to wide acclaim in 1969. She is the recipient of many awards and honors in poetry, here and in England.

BROWSING COLLECTION
14-DAY CHECKOUT
No Holds • No Renewals

TOUCHED

Also by Walter Mosley

Easy Rawlins Mysteries

Blood Grove	*Cinnamon Kiss*	*A Little Yellow Dog*
Charcoal Joe	*Little Scarlet*	*Black Betty*
Rose Gold	*Six Easy Pieces*	*White Butterfly*
Little Green	*Bad Boy Brawly Brown*	*A Red Death*
Blonde Faith	*Gone Fishin'*	*Devil in a Blue Dress*

Leonid McGill Mysteries

Trouble Is What I Do	*Karma*
And Sometimes I Wonder About You	*Known to Evil*
All I Did Was Shoot My Man	*The Long Fall*
When the Thrill Is Gone	

Other Fiction

Every Man a King	*Fortunate Son*
The Awkward Black Man	*The Wave*
Down the River unto the Sea	*47*
John Woman	*The Man in My Basement*
Debbie Doesn't Do It Anymore	*Fear Itself*
Stepping Stone / Love Machine	*Futureland: Nine Stories of an Imminent World*
Merge / Disciple	
The Gift of Fire / On the Head of a Pin	*Fearless Jones*
The Last Days of Ptolemy Grey	*Walkin' the Dog*
The Tempest Tales	*Blue Light*
The Right Mistake	*Always Outnumbered, Always Outgunned*
Diablerie	*RL's Dream*
Killing Johnny Fry	
Fear of the Dark	

Original Ebooks

The Further Adventures of Tempest Landry	*Parishioner*	*Odyssey*

Nonfiction

Elements of Fiction	*This Year You Write Your Novel*
Folding the Red into the Black	*Life Out of Context*
The Graphomaniac's Primer	*What Next: A Memoir Toward World Peace*
Twelve Steps Toward Political Revelation	*Workin' on the Chain Gang*

Plays
The Fall of Heaven

TOUCHED

A NOVEL

WALTER
MOSLEY

Atlantic Monthly Press
New York

FIRST EDITION

Published simultaneously in Canada
Printed in the United States of America

First Grove Atlantic hardcover edition: October 2023

Library of Congress Cataloging-in-Publication data is available for this title.

ISBN 978-0-8021-6184-0
eISBN 978-0-8021-6185-7

Atlantic Monthly Press
an imprint of Grove Atlantic
154 West 14th Street
New York, NY 10011

Distributed by Publishers Group West

groveatlantic.com

23 24 25 26   10 9 8 7 6 5 4 3 2 1

TOUCHED

I awoke on a Saturday morning with the Plan fully formed, but fading, in my mind. Nothing else had changed. It was as if I had gone to sleep years before, contemplating a tricky conundrum, and remained in that doze until the knotty question had been completely disentangled—at least mentally so, at least for a while.

But when I awoke it was merely the next morning, as if time had folded back on itself, depositing me where I was before.

Tessa was in bed next to me, sound asleep. Her hair was wrapped in violet nylon netting. She'd sleep for two more hours. Brown would certainly be asleep in his room and Celestine, whom everyone called Seal, was probably sitting in her bed reading a library book.

I sat up and took a deep breath that felt like my first inhalation in a very long time.

Cells began to fire in my body. That's the only way I can describe it. It was as if my physiology had also undergone some kind of transformation. I could feel my organs and glands pumping out chemicals, altering tissue and even bone.

There had been an azure plane where beings, not human, had poked and butted me, fondled and fucked me in ways that made no sense in the earthly realm. I was there and others were too, other people, human beings, being prepared for something, for some things. It occurred to me that we were not all in accordance. Our Plans were different and sometimes even at odds. There were 107 assigned to the Great Change, but our tasks often seemed to contradict one another.

One hundred and seven human beings conditioned and trained to prepare for the Transition. But there were other creatures too; other earthly lifeforms that were there to complete us—or maybe we were there to complete them or, even more accurately, to complete a circuit, a turning, a revolution.

It was only on that Saturday morning, with Tessa sleeping next to me and the sun slanting in through the seam of our heavy curtains, that I understood the Plan in its totality. And even then, while I was rousing from my centuries-long sleep, the lessons I had learned were receding into the shelves and cubby-holes of my unconscious mind.

I can remember only some of it now, after the first skirmish in an intergalactic invasion. There was a place that gave the impression of many shades of blue, but I can't say if my eyes were working there. I was aware of different beings from a vast range of planes and realities. They spoke to me but in ways that transformed rather than informed me. They were like a congress that met only once, decided on the fates of worlds, and then disbanded when their words, their annunciations, had been received and digested.

My world, they said, was wrong. It, the planet itself, had spawned a disease of which I was a part. This contagion had begun to multiply and it had to be rendered impotent—by any means necessary.

I was to be an antibody in the eradication of this rampant syndrome. I was the cure or, more precisely, a cure.

And there were others who were being modified, as I was, to rid Earth of the danger of the genetic disorder of humankind—107 men and women refashioned to save the universe from the biology and resultant technology of evil.

There were 107 different plans, some radically diverse.

As I climbed out of bed the memories began to retreat. I knew that everything was different but I could no longer name the various other treatments (106 human beings), our agreements, and our therapeutic conflicts.

Throwing open the drapes, I forgot these serious issues and grinned broadly at the flood of sunlight.

I slid open the glass door to our second-floor deck and walked outside feeling that I was entering the world, committing to a battle like any foot soldier given his orders, obeying because that was my conditioning and my duty.

Mr. Snyder's oak tree swayed in the morning breeze. There was the smell of fuel in the air and of food cooking.

"Mama, look!" a child shouted, but for me, at that moment, it was just one of the myriad sensations of this old/new world.

I had been a petty human when I had fallen asleep a thousand years ago but now I was something else.

One hundred and seven ways to change the world and no two of them in exact accordance. How could this end well? Beyond the chill on my skin and the chemicals in the air, I could feel the vibration of souls all around. Errant and leaky, confused and starving— the souls of insects and trees, humans and other mammals all drawn to the impossible hope of unity.

This notion of harmony arrested my worries. I had been in a place where there had been agreement among differences, something beyond love and understanding. I closed my eyes and imagined this pristine moment as if maybe it was a gaudy, rainbow-colored barge sailing off, leaving only the hope of something that had always been an impossible dream.

Standing out in that early morning, I knew it was my job to recall that amazing notion and to make everyone in the world aware.

I don't know how long I stood like that, with the notion of the absolute fading from my mind but at the same time exhilarating my heart.

"Marty," she said.

I turned to see my wife of a millennium ago. She was dark brown in a blue-and-green kimono. Beautiful, almost forgotten, it seemed impossible that she stood there.

"What are you doing?" she asked.

"Today?" I inquired.

Did she know what my mission was? Was she one of the crusaders? I realized then that I had never had a physical impression of my fellow missionaries.

"Standing out here naked," she said, "and look at your, your thing."

I was naked and had become aroused sexually when I saw Tessa. The wind and sun felt good on my skin. The air in my lungs was rich and lush.

"There's a change coming," I said. There was an odd lilt to my words; an accent developed during the centuries away.

"What?"

I took a step toward her and reached out to take her by the wrist.

Tessa was afraid but she was also worried. While pulling her wrist away, she moved her shoulder toward me. It was a language older than humanity coming from the poetry of the genetic soul.

"Hold it right there!" a man shouted.

If I had been back for just a few more days, maybe just a few more hours, I would have been able to decipher the threat in those words. But my body had not finished with its internal makeover and the old world was new to me again—alien.

"God is not a being," I said to my wife. "It is an ever-recurring, never-the-same meeting of entities that come together, not unlike the myth of the primal atom."

"What?" she asked while looking over the deck at something on the lawn below.

"I said, don't move!" came the voice again.

Tessa was looking at the origin of the command. Without letting her go, I turned my head in that direction.

There were two people in similar garments, a man and a woman, with weapons held high and pointed at me.

I stared at them, trying to make the proper associations, straining to understand what these two humans had to do with eternity.

While the woman kept a bead on me, the man, with great dexterity, climbed on top of our picnic

7

table and hopped over the short railing surrounding our deck. He pulled out his gun again.

Tessa shouted and pulled away from me.

She moved toward the policeman, who was the color of bronze, but short. I don't know why I thought a man of that coloring should be . . . larger.

"Get on your knees!" the bronze man said as he pushed Tessa to the side, out of the line of fire.

I noticed a woman and a girl-child standing in the yard next door. The woman was trying to keep the child from looking. It was then that I realized I still had the erection.

"On your knees!"

Was I being arrested for my erection? No. It was more complex than that.

I looked up a bit and saw Los Angeles down the hill from our second-floor balcony. The view was majestic to my human sense of proportions and, at the same time, quaint, almost miniscule, to the vision that had grown, was growing, inside me while simultaneously hiding the Plan from my consciousness.

I felt an impact against the side of my head and gravity took over from my natural biological resistance. That, I thought, was one of the keys to the threat of humankind. We, the elements of life, resist the natural flow of things. Aggression was part of the essence of biological life. This genetic irrationality was inherited from the first viruses that spawned in the warm pools of Early Earth.

Tessa screamed.

"Daddy!" Brown yelled.

"Stay back!" the cop hollered.

"Are you all right?" the female cop, an Asian woman, shouted. She was talking to my wife.

"Daddy!" Seal—Celestine—cried.

I went limp trying to counteract the gyre of escalating violence that I seemed to be causing. Or maybe it was the blow to my head that was slowing my mind. At any rate, darkness engulfed the multitude of thoughts associated with my consciousness, paring them down to a dark cavity below the surface of perception.

I awoke for the second time since my reincarnation.

I was in a short bed with a soft mattress beneath me, swaddled in a straitjacket that was bound to that bed.

9

". . . but he was just sleepwalking, and the cops attacked him," a woman was saying.

"He resisted arrest," a man responded. "He's going to have to stand trial, at least go before a judge."

"Fine," the woman relented, "but let him go home."

"We can't."

"Mr. Just has never even been arrested for speeding," the woman said. "What is the reasoning behind incarcerating him?"

"It is procedure to arrest the suspected perpetrator concerning any complaint of a sexual nature having to do with children."

"What complaint?"

"He was naked and sexually aroused in front of a nine-year-old girl."

"He was on the balcony of his own home, sleepwalking."

"In plain sight of a nine-year-old girl."

There were chemicals in my veins; I could taste them. Allowed enough time, I could have given them names on the Great List of the Moments of Existence as detailed by the Celestial Congress that anointed me "The Cure." There were others on the list: The Answer, The Final Solution, The Gift of Laughter, and many more, most of which I had forgotten.

I sighed and sat upright.

"What's going on?"

"Martin Just?" a man in a too-green suit asked me. He was what they call a Caucasian—a white man thirty pounds overweight and suffering from more than just the disease of mortality.

"Yes?"

"I am placing you under arrest for resisting an officer of the law and for lewd public display."

"What's your name and rank?" I asked.

This question irked the middle-aged cop.

"Detective Thomas O'Halloran," he said. "Benson?"

Two uniformed policemen, one obviously named Benson, came into the room.

"Get him dressed, down to the precinct, and booked," Detective O'Halloran declared.

"This isn't right," the woman speaker said.

She was maybe thirty, in a bright-red dress designed for a party and not a legal debate. Her heavy features kept her from being classically beautiful, but she was magnetic and there was a powerful, animalistic life force pulsing inside her.

"Take it up with the judge in the morning, Ms. Clayborn," O'Halloran said.

"This man does not deserve to be thrown in jail," the woman called Ms. Clayborn protested.

"Where are Tessa and the kids?" I asked.

The cop and lawyer turned their heads toward me.

"It's late," the woman told me. "Visiting hours are over and you've been sequestered at any rate."

"What's your name?" I asked the woman while the policemen worked on untying my restraints.

"Lena, Lena Clayborn," she said. "I'm your lawyer."

"I broke the law?" This idea struck a chord of fear in my core. It had nothing to do with petty human laws or morals. It was the possibility that I might fail in my duty that brought on mortal dread.

"You didn't do anything wrong, Mr. Just," the lawyer said. "This is simply a misunderstanding that has gotten out of hand."

"Put these on," one of the uniformed policemen ordered.

He was holding out a pale-green hospital outfit; loose pants and a jacket-like shirt with mid-forearm sleeves.

I reached for the clothing and noticed how dark my skin was compared to that of the other people in the room. I was reminded then that I was a Black man. This was once a very important detail of my life, inordinately so. My coloring defined a place among others that was varied and inconsistent but rarely a benefit. Race had made me at once different and part of an imagined whole.

"You might want to leave while the man gets dressed," O'Halloran said to the female lawyer.

"I'm staying with my client as long as possible."

I hustled on my pants and pulled on the cotton shirt.

"Where's your shoes?" the second uniform asked.

"I don't know," I said.

Standing in the garish whiteness of the fluorescent-lit hospital room, I was trying to maintain balance. My body was still changing while the images in my mind were dissipating. I woke up hours before, in my own bed, certain in my knowledge of God, but this certainty was slowly devolving into a kind

13

of disorganized belief system. I was under arrest for having an erection and I was a Black man, whatever that was supposed to mean.

"Under the bed," O'Halloran said to me.

There was a pair of green paper slippers on the floor. I stepped into them.

"Paper shoes?" my lawyer said.

"If you'll excuse me, Ms. Clayborn," the detective replied. "I will be taking my prisoner into custody."

In handcuffs, I was put behind a cage wall in the back seat of a police car. I sat there, distracted by the complexity of my situation.

I had been sent, or maybe even created, to change the world by my being. My body chemistry and the ideas that sailed across the mirror of my mind had been recrafted to save existence, in all of its iterations, from a world tainted by the scum that the living gene produced.

I was not, however, a destroyer. My job was to rehabilitate, to repair the juncture between pure being and transitory life. I had no reason to be arrested and treated like an enemy—even if I was an enemy of sorts.

*   *   *

"We got a real winner for you here, McKenzie," the cop whose name was Benny said.

"Oh?" uttered the big man behind the high desk. He looked down on me with diseased gray eyes.

"Yeah. This guy here decided to show his big black hard-on to a nine-year-old white girl."

"Huh," the bulbous admissions cop grunted. He was looking at me closely. This attention, more than anything so far, brought me back into the life that had seemed so far in the past.

"Yeah," Benny said. "And his lawyer got O'Halloran to sign off on isolation."

"Really?" the man named McKenzie speculated. "Too bad we're having so much overcrowding. Must be the full moon. But I'll try and work something out."

There was a sinister inflection to the admissions cop's tone.

I was dragged off and put in a small cell behind an iron door and left there to sit on a thin mattress laid upon a shelf that jutted from the wall.

The lighting was dim, but I didn't mind that. I hoped that Tessa and the kids were okay. I wondered if I would be allowed to accomplish some part of my mission.

There were insects in the walls; I could feel them scuttling. There was suffering in the general vicinity. I sensed men, and some women—many in almost catatonic trauma—waiting for something to come.

I was that something. I knew it.

There was an aluminum toilet and a sink the size of a soup bowl nestled in the corner of the narrow cell. I urinated and drank from the spigot.

The door came open a few minutes later and a huge man was ushered in by three baton-bearing guards.

The man was taller than I by at least four inches (making him somewhere around six foot four) and he outweighed me by sixty pounds or more. He wore only jeans and laceless leather shoes with no socks. His bare torso had dozens of tattoos scrawled across it; crosses and naked women, obscure script and one big red swastika. He was bald and heavy with muscle.

"Get off the cot, nigger," he said after we were left alone. "That's mine."

I didn't consider the request. I just did what he said. I moved toward the door and sat in the corner on the floor while he thumped his heavy bulk down on the mattress.

The man smelled strongly of sweat. I found the odor calming and somewhat transportive. I closed my eyes and thought about being human, about living and sweating and straining against the inevitable. I was a hopeless cause; all living things were. We lived for no reason but were passionate about our reproduction and survival. We tried so hard and offered almost nothing to existence. This impossible task seemed somehow hopeful . . .

"There soap in the sink?"

He was staring at me. I realized that he was trying to intimidate me. He was like McKenzie at the admissions desk. He hated me for a set of reasons laid out by a pointless history.

"I don't know," I said.

"You better hope so," he told me. "'Cause if not your asshole is gonna bleed bad."

"What?"

"Come ovah here and get down on your knees."

I stood up then and he did too.

"I said, on your knees."

I understood what was happening, the menace of the tattooed man, but my mind was in too many places to perceive him as the sole threat I should have been concentrating on. He was just an aspect of the disease for which I was the cure.

"Did you hear me?" the man asked.

I didn't answer, nor did I lower to my knees. I can't say for sure why I didn't obey. It seemed as if there was no alternative. But I just stood there.

Moving faster than I would have suspected possible, he grabbed me with both hands around my throat.

Choking me hard, he pulled my face to his. I could smell the rank breath of mortality.

"Suck dick or die," he whispered.

I felt my eyes bulging and the panic of suffocation firing at the back of my brain, but emotionally I was distant. Even as consciousness fled, I was amazed by the smell of humanity.

*   *   *

When I awoke the third time since my return to this plane, I was once again in a hospital room, once again restrained in a straitjacket.

A man and woman, both clad in white, were looking down on me. He was a white man and she, brown-skinned.

"You're awake?" the man asked.

My hands ached.

"Yes," I said. "What happened?"

"You don't remember?"

"I was in a jail cell . . ."

"Do you remember what happened there?" the woman asked.

"They brought in this big, sweaty guy. He liked me and didn't."

The man and the woman looked at each other, sharing a thought that I was not privy to.

"Excuse me," the man said. "I'm supposed to call the police when you regain consciousness."

They may have gone to report my awakening to the police, I don't know. But for a very long time I was left alone in the white room. There were no windows and

19

few sounds. I was losing the direct knowledge of my millennium of training and conditioning. All I was left with was a sense of faith that I had been among the Chosen.

My hands hurt but I couldn't see them because my arms were bound tightly to my sides.

The restraints didn't bother me. For almost my entire time away I was only a flicker of consciousness with no bodily awareness. I was as the superior beings were: a part of everything, existence with awareness but rarely a motive.

I urinated in my hospital pants because no one came to relieve me.

After many hours, four brawny orderlies came. I was cursed for my bodily functions, then unbound, thrown under a cold shower, dressed in hospital whites, and strapped back into restraints.

They, all four men, dragged me down a hall to an alleyway where I was thrown into a gray van and driven to another paved aisle. I was handed over to four men in uniforms, who led me to a small room where I was made to sit in a square-cut metal chair that was soldered to the floor.

"Where am I?" I asked one of the guards as he chained my left ankle to the chair.

The ugly man (he was light brown and unhappy) stood and said, "Keep your mouth shut and you won't get hit."

For the next hour or so I wondered if it was my fate to work on the world from a prison cell. Maybe the authorities had figured out my assignment and decided I was to be executed. Why else would they put so many guards on me? I was somewhat tall but not physically imposing.

They must have known somehow that I was a threat to the mindless hegemony of genetic life and its unconscious machinations.

But how could they? I was asleep in my bed next to my wife. I was a simple salesman for an upscale computer service company—nobody from nowhere.

When the door came open again, the same four guards unshackled my foot and led me to an elevator. As we descended, the doors opened and a woman tried to get in, but the lead guard held up a hand and told her, "Prisoner transport. Take the next car."

We exited into a wide hallway crowded with people. From the high windows I could tell that it was daytime. People stared at me. I suppose I looked dangerous and demented.

All around me, human souls shimmered and shivered inside their husks. I wanted to succor them but could not.

The phalanx of guards pushed through a set of large double doors and I was ushered into a crowded courtroom.

"Marty!" It was Tessa. She was standing next to an aisle seat in the gallery, wearing a blue dress and rose-colored pearls that I'd given her a thousand years ago. She reached out for me.

"Stand back, ma'am," the light-colored guard said.

In an instant I hated him.

"Your honor," Lena Clayborn was saying. "It is extremely prejudicial for the district attorney to have my client brought before the court trussed up like a Thanksgiving turkey. This is a man who has never been arrested or even suspected of a crime before two days ago."

I had stopped to look at my wife. The guards were pushing me forward. I had to urinate again. The courtroom was filled with spectators. I'd never been before a judge but it seemed that there was more at stake than a simple case of a man standing naked somewhere outside.

"Your honor," a big man in an ochre suit said, raising his voice above an imagined din. "This man is extremely dangerous. He was originally arrested for sexual deviance involving a child, and now charges of aggravated assault and second-degree murder have been added. He killed a man with his bare hands before the guards could stop him."

His last words reminded me of how much my hands hurt.

"My client was arrested for sleepwalking in the nude on his own deck," Lena Clayborn said. "He was thrown in an eight-by-six-foot jail cell with a man six inches taller and a hundred pounds heavier than him. This man had already served seven and a half years for manslaughter. He was a member of a radical white brotherhood and has a long and bloody history of documented racial hate crimes. And as far as the guards are concerned, they didn't find the body until the next morning, and my client was on the floor, bruised about the neck and unconscious."

What was the man's name? I wondered. How was he killed? Were my painful hands the evidence?

The judge was a tiny white woman with intense black eyes. She stared at me.

"Mr. Just?"

"Yes, your honor," I said civilly.

"What do you have to say for yourself?"

"I woke up, at least I thought I did, from a very deep sleep. I'd had a long and convoluted dream and I guess I was still processing everything I'd experienced . . . dreamt. I walked outside, and after a while my wife came out to see what was wrong. Then the police came. I was confused and they, this one officer, hit me with his pistol and then they took me to jail. I was locked in a cell and then this big guy was put in with me. He told me to get on my knees and when I didn't, he started choking me. The next thing I knew I was in a straitjacket . . . again. The first time I was knocked out they put me in restraints too. And now I hear that I'm being charged with murder. It feels like I never woke up, your honor."

The words I spoke were in a way instinctual. There was a baseline consciousness in my brain that could speak almost without my volition. It was like another persona, a man I once wanted to be, nestled in the folds of my brain, who was there to come out and protect me in the world of deterioration and disease.

"The defendant sounds perfectly normal to me, Mr. Trapas," the judge said to the man representing the district attorney's office.

"His hands were covered in the victim's blood," the fat blond prosecutor said.

"He was also unconscious, with bruises in the shape of fingers on his throat," my lawyer responded.

"Untie Mr. Just," the judge decreed.

My four keepers worked deftly on the restraints and in less than a minute I was free. The first thing I noticed was that my knuckles were swollen and bloody. They itched. The second thing to come to me was the silence of the room. Everyone was staring at me. Maybe they were expecting Mr. Hyde to manifest himself and start throwing people around like the ragdolls they were.

"How are you feeling, Mr. Just?" the judge asked.

"Like I can breathe."

"I'm sure. Are you angry?"

"No. There's a lot going on in my mind but I'm not mad at anybody."

"Are you guilty of the charges against you?"

"Your honor," Lena Clayborn protested.

"Mr. Just?" the judge insisted.

"I did walk out on my deck naked. They say I was sleepwalking. Maybe I wasn't asleep, but I wasn't thinking about being naked either. I wouldn't do that again. As far as killing that man . . . All I remember is him choking me."

"Bail, Mr. Trapas?" the judge asked, still looking at me.

"We think Mr. Just should be remanded, at least until we know if he's a threat or not."

"Martin Just has a full-time job, a worried wife, and two children," Clayborn said. "He's a taxpaying homeowner who maintains his innocence."

"When the police found him, he had the victim's blood on his hands, Judge Jeremy," fat Trapas intoned.

These words riveted me. He meant them as some kind of gut-wrenching metaphor. It was his job to

keep the bloody murderer behind bars. His seem-
ingly straightforward statement was intended to paint
a picture for the court, an image that would convict
me then and there at the arraignment.

I was aware of the aggressive intentions behind
his claim, but that was not what enthralled me.

It was the image of blood on the greatest tool
that evolution has ever produced—the hand. I had
no doubt that my hands had taken a man's life; the
pain in my knuckles attested to that. We all had bloody
hands. We were all killers if any of us were. We were
all guilty. This was the hopeless state of animal life
and also of our deep ignorance. The idea that there
could be a court trying to assign guilt amid a world
comprised of the guilty called up an overpowering
grief. It was all I could do not to groan out loud.

"If this man is a danger, he must be kept in cus-
tody," Trapas was saying. He was a young man in spite
of his girth.

"I understand—" Judge Jeremy said.

"No," Tessa cried from behind me.

"—but," the judge continued, "I cannot in good
conscience put Mr. Just back in jail when there is no
compelling evidence against him. As far as I can see

he did not solicit, nor was he aware of, the child's attention, and there is no witness to the fight in the jail cell. I am here to protect the people, but I am also responsible for the rights of the accused. I am letting Mr. Just go home on his own recognizance. A pretrial date will be set by the court."

They didn't let me go immediately. I was taken to a locked room, where District Attorney Fyodor Trapas and his associate, Melanie Blythe, explained to me and my lawyer the terms of my release passed down by the court, the police, and the district attorney's office.

Trapas took the judge's ruling as an insult, and for this he blamed me. He had a sour look on his face and his soul reeked of hatred, actual hatred, for me.

"We expect you to be available to the court and the police as the investigation continues," Ms. Blythe said to the space between me and Lena Clayborn. She, Blythe, was a young Black woman in peacock blue.

The hue of her dress reminded me of my time in azure.

"He will be at his home or his job," Lena said.

Glancing at my lawyer, I thought that maybe her nose had been broken at one time.

"If you run I will put you in jail until 2050," Trapas warned.

"Why do you hate me?" the real me asked.

I say "the real me" because the template of a related but alternate personality had been laid upon my psyche. This false or alternate persona had been formed during my thousand-year rest in order to protect me from betraying my mission. But the guardian personality wasn't complete—it couldn't be, because I, the real me, had been chosen for my natural proclivities. My . . . creators needed me to be free from domination.

"You're scum, Just. You're a child molester and a murderer, and I'm going to see that you stay in prison until you're too old to be a threat to anyone ever again."

Fyodor Trapas's neck bulged out over the collar of his shirt and he took breaths in sudden gasps. Looking at his pale white skin and jade-green eyes, I had a vision of a young man standing over a woman's prostrate form. She was either unconscious or dead.

The man, who had no definite features, was looking at his hands—there was blood on the palms.

"I'm not you, Fyodor," the man inside me said while forcing me to look Trapas in the eye.

"Why you—"

Fyodor Trapas lunged across the table, throwing a punch as he did so.

In a trance of lucidity I stood up and quickly moved six feet back toward the wall, allowing the portly man to fall. He landed hard on his gut and was winded by the belly flop.

I raised my hands above my head as both women shouted.

Three uniformed policemen burst through the door. One of them grabbed my upheld right arm and twisted it behind my back. I had the feeling that I was allowing the cop to manhandle me so—that if I had wanted to I could have lifted him up over my head and thrown him against his friends.

It was when I had this exhilarating thought that I began to suspect I had gone insane. I mean, I had no proof that I'd left my body overnight and traveled to a place beyond distance and time. I was experiencing (maybe suffering) strange perceptions that were in no way corroborated by practical knowledge. So what if I got Trapas angry? He was an angry man before I spoke.

"Stop!" Melanie Blythe shouted. "Mr. Trapas just fell over, that's all."

The other two policemen were helping the fat DA to his feet. He was gulping air now.

"That right?" one of the policemen, a tall and skinny youth, asked.

"Yeah, yeah," Trapas gasped. "I leaned over too far and fell. Guess I need to lose a few pounds."

"Do you want to press charges?" Lena asked me.

"For what?" my template replied. "Like the man said, he just fell."

I was brought to a room where Tessa was waiting.

"Where are the kids?" were my first words.

Instead of answering, Tessa grabbed me fiercely, clamping her arms around my neck. The violence of this desperate but loving act brought to mind the man I had been charged with killing. He had grabbed me around the neck. He had felt a passion in his breast. I sensed a brief hint of need coming from him just before I lost control and my template took over.

"Marty, Marty," my wife cried.

I put my arms around her. Lena Clayborn was standing there watching us.

"What was his name?" I asked the lawyer while holding my wife.

"Fyodor Trapas."

"No. Not the lawyer—the, the man they say I killed. I don't remember it."

"Lon Farthey."

"Marty," Tessa said. "Talk to me. Tell me what's going on."

"Let's sit down, honey."

There were four plastic chairs set around a green metal table. All three of us sat. Tessa took hold of my hands and held them like a mother wanting to restrain a child. She was looking into my eyes as I had done with Fyodor Trapas.

I remembered that face.

When I had awakened in the bed, Tessa was merely an expectation. For centuries, it felt, I had been a bodiless intelligence. At the end of that time Tessa's name and face were shown to me. Her name and our relationship were . . . posited.

I expected her to be there but felt no relationship, not at first.

But in that small debriefing room I began to feel her, to remember how close we had been.

"What's wrong, Marty?" she asked. "Why are you looking at me like that?"

"It was the dream, Tess," I said.

"What dream?"

"I can't explain it."

"Was it some kind of nightmare?"

"It was, it was like leaving my body. I was allowed to see or perceive, but I no longer had a motive."

"Mr. Just," Lena Clayborn said.

"Yes?" I was still looking into Tessa's soft and worried brown eyes.

"Your pretrial begins in two weeks. At that time the court will decide if there is enough evidence to try you. The coroner is examining Farthey's body now. We need to have a talk concerning everything that you remember."

Tessa squeezed my hands. They ached under the pressure.

"Could I just go home and get a good night's sleep?" I asked. "You know I'm very disoriented."

"Are you all right, Mr. Just?" The tone of the lawyer's voice caused me to turn to her.

I got an impression of her aura . . . That was the word that occurred to me—aura. It wasn't a surrounding luminescence but like a space I could intuit by letting the rest of my senses ease.

Clayborn was worried that I was actually insane, that if I went home, I might harm my family.

"Do you think you should go see a doctor?" she was asking me.

"I don't know everything that happened in that jail cell, counselor," I, or maybe my template, said. "But I do know that he threatened me and attacked me and if I did anything to him it was because I was defending myself."

"Let's go home, Marty," Tessa said. She stood up, still holding onto my hands.

The lawyer was watching my eyes. She might have seen something that worried her. But then she shrugged.

"Your wife is right, Mr. Just," the lawyer told me. "Go home. Get some sleep, and when you wake up, call me at my office. Tessa has all my information."

"What happened, Dad?" Brown asked. He was seventeen, with a heavy face and somewhat ethereal eyes, short and squat like my father and mother and prone to passion—like Tessa.

"How come you went outside with no clothes on in the first place?" Celestine asked. Two years younger than her brother, she was the darkest skinned of us all, nearly black, with dominant African features.

"Leave your father alone," Tessa said. "He's been through a terrible ordeal and he needs to rest."

We were eating pepperoni pizza in the den. Tessa had decided to serve the delivery dinner there rather than in the dining room because it was cozier. For most of the meal we talked about how the kids were doing in school, but Brown couldn't avoid the subject that was on all our minds.

"I just want to know what happened at the jail. You didn't really hurt anybody, did you?"

I had always been a mild-mannered man. Raised in the Boston suburb Newton Highlands, I was of the American middle class, with all the urbanity, timidity, and so-called sophistication that came with it.

"I don't remember what happened in there, B," I said. "The police say that I was in a fight, but I don't remember."

"How could you not remember somethin' like that, Dad?" my son asked, lifting his hands and shoulders.

"Brown!" Tessa said in her sternest voice. She was from the wrong side of Detroit and was the disciplinarian of the family. I had never hit either of my children.

"I think I was in a state of shock," I said to my son. Tessa flashed her angry look at me.

"You know," I continued, ignoring her stare, "that policeman hit me in the head and then I was thrown into a jail cell. They were saying that I had done something terrible to a child and so the police were all mad at me. And that Farthey man with that red swastika tattooed on his chest—"

"Marty," Tessa said. "We don't need to talk about it now. You have to get some rest."

The kids were both looking at me, a little startled by the dynamic at the table. I couldn't blame them. Their world had been knocked off its foundation. If Tessa had been arrested, it would have been more understandable. She was the wild, hot-blooded one. She might go to jail or kill somebody with her bare hands—but not me.

I was the one who would try to reason with a burglar or forgive someone who struck me.

"Your mother's right," I said. "We should get a good night's sleep and talk about this after the dust has had time to settle. I'm home and that's all that matters."

In the bedroom I took off my clothes while Tessa changed into her pink nightgown. She was in her mid-thirties and used to being with me. She had a shapely figure and her breasts stood up under the soft cotton. I could see her nipples and, even with all that I'd been through, I became aroused again.

"You've got to be kidding me," she said in a tone that would put a damper on any man's hard-on.

"Come here," I—or, more accurately, the template of the man I always wanted to be—said.

"What?" There was uncertainty and maybe a little excitement in Tessa's tone.

"I said come here."

I sat down on the little padded bench that stood in front of her makeup table.

Tessa took two steps toward me and stopped.

"I don't know what's gotten into you, Marty, but—"

I stood up quickly and she stopped talking. Reaching down, I lifted the hem of her nightgown and then picked her up by her buttocks. When I lowered her it was onto my full erection.

"Marty!" she cried.

It wasn't me—that's what I wanted to tell her. It wasn't me but the man created from the stuff of my desires now called upon to protect me. He had seen my wife and for a moment taken over my actions.

Slowly, with great strength, he lifted and lowered her with mechanical syncopation. She gripped my shoulder and moaned in my ear. I continued the motions until she came and then I did. Then I carried her to the bed and lowered her.

"Take off that nightgown," I said, standing over her and still erect.

"Marty, what's gotten into you?"

"Take it off."

I fucked my wife for hours. That's the truth. In our many years together I had been loving and attentive, always attracted to my firecracker wife. I had made love to her many nights. Sometimes we may have simply had sex. But that night I fucked that woman like a drunken sailor on leave—in wartime.

"Baby, you got to give it a rest," she whispered when I hovered over her again.

"I need you," Temple said with my vocal chords. I named him that night.

"Your little girl is sore," she said in an unusually conciliatory tone. "She needs some rest."

My breath was coming fast and I was still hard and ready.

"Please, baby," Tessa said.

That was when the transition occurred. Looking at Tessa through Temple's eyes, there was a shift in my awareness and suddenly I was in control again. There was the feeling of an emotional vacuum or maybe a lessening of pressure inside my head.

"Did I hurt you?" I asked.

"You hurt me good," she said with a smile that I had never elicited before.

She kissed me and pulled me down next to her.

"I didn't believe that you could have even been in a fight before tonight, Martin." She also had a name for my alter ego—not Marty but Martin, not a boy but a man.

"Yeah," I said. "Maybe that dream drove me insane."

"Tell me about this dream." Tessa turned to me, her breast resting on my shoulder.

I was a different man, and that man became aroused by a woman he had been watching have wild sex with another.

"No, Martin," she said. "I told you I'm worn out."

Taking in a deep breath I closed my eyes, trying to remember my dream while forgetting desire.

"I, I fell asleep like I usually do—imagining that I was transported somehow to Superman's Fortress of Solitude—"

"That's how you fall asleep?" Tessa asked. She put her hand on my chest.

"If you don't want more sex, you can't touch me like that," I said.

"Oh," she said shyly, pulling her hand away. "Sorry."

"I never told you about my fantasy?"

"No. What's a fortress of solitude like?"

"It's located in the North Pole and is impregnable. I imagine being there, and that makes me feel safe. No one and nothing can get to me there."

"Sounds like a good place to go on vacation."

"Usually I only have to think about being there and I go right to sleep. But the other night I didn't fall off immediately. I walked around the place, looking at the odd plants and the little city in a five-gallon glass jar. I had been wandering around for a while marveling at the amazing collection of alien artifacts when I became aware that this wasn't *my* dream."

"What do you mean, not yours?"

"It's like I started out in my dream and then wandered into another reality. You know, like walking through a door in your own home and coming out in the house next door."

Tessa sat up and peered into my eyes. "Like you left your own mind?"

"I found this long corridor that was formed from a yellow metal, but not gold. I walked for ages. Finally I got to a large room where there was this huge pile of glowing blue stones. The pile was as big as a small hill. You know, like the one the kids go climbing on at Griffith Park. And I became aware that the hill was alive."

"Wow. That's some dream."

"That was only the beginning. I realized that the hill had an odor or a vibration, maybe it was like radiation—ultraviolet rays or something like that. Anyway, I knew that there was intelligent communication being imparted to me but I had to learn the language. It took a very, very long time."

Decades. I sat down before that blue hill and thought for so long that my body died and turned to dust. I didn't tell Tessa that part. When I arose I was pure spirit—ready to receive my lesson.

"And what did the mountain have to say?" Tessa asked.

These words shocked me back to awareness.

"That I was the cure," I said.

"The cure for what?"

"Man is only an early step in a complex viral system."

"Viral system? What are you talking about?" Tessa was an office manager for Klega Toys International but she trained as a nurse. At one point she had even considered becoming a doctor.

"We are innately a self-mutilating race," I said. "It starts out with tattoos and scarification, pacemakers and false limbs. But that will soon give way to mechanical implants combined with gene-splicing techniques. In just ten thousand years individual human beings will expand their physical selves to the size of moons—even planets."

"That's what you dreamed about?"

"Biology resists the pull of gravity," I quoted from a sermon given by a pile of blue rock. "We see meaning in this resistance. At first it doesn't seem like anything serious. The universe continues its gyre and nothing is different. But if the infection of DNA moves to the level of interstellar domination, the natural flow of things will be thrown off. Sentience older than a billion trillion reiterations of existence will simply cease to be."

"And you're the cure?" Tessa asked.

"I don't really remember," I said truthfully. "All I know is that there are one hundred and seven alternatives that, when combined or pitted against each other, represent millions of scenarios that would stop the onset of oblivion."

"My stomach feels funny," Tessa said.

"The power of the mind is greater than even our greatest thinkers have surmised," I said as if in answer to her complaint. "We can recreate ourselves to a great degree by thought alone."

"Could you get me some Bromo?" she said.

Temple laid my left hand on her head while placing my right palm on her lower abdomen. She lay back under this pressure.

"Your hands are hot," Tessa whispered. "That feels good. Real good."

She passed out soon after. I sat there looking at her through another man's eyes. It was an odd experience. At that point in our development, Temple and I were unable to communicate directly. He had his job and I had mine. It was possible, even likely, that I had had a schizophrenic breakdown during my long dream. Temple was a made-up persona who had a lusty appetite and hot hands.

Tessa writhed under my touch, responding to some internal chemistry.

I sat there next to her, between this world and a place that probably did not exist.

"Your mother has a fever," I said to Seal at the breakfast table just after six thirty the next morning. "Probably all the excitement."

"You need me to stay home with her, Daddy?" she asked, looking up from her book.

"No, baby, just look in on her and make sure she takes some aspirin."

"Are you okay, Daddy?"

I took a deep breath and then exhaled before saying, "You know? I think I'm all right. Everything that happened feels like a dream."

"Wasn't it a dream that started all this?"

"What are you reading?"

"*One Hundred Years of Solitude* by Gabriel García Márquez."

"Is it good?"

"I don't really get it, but it's fun."

I went to the room I use as my home office and searched the Internet for information on myself and the crimes I had committed. Seven articles, sixty-two blog posts, and four video news reports were immediately available.

A lot of the information was erroneous or mere supposition, but there were some interesting ideas. An online TV news outlet quoted an anonymous police source as saying that Lon Farthey had been bludgeoned to death, that the habitual criminal had taken a terrible beating.

If this account was true, I thought, then it had to be someone else who fought with Farthey. Physically he was my superior and obviously an abler fighter than I. I didn't have the strength or the nature to inflict such damage.

That's when I thought of Temple.

I didn't have the strength or inclination to lift my wife up and down like I was some kind of mindless oil derrick . . .

I went to the front door to retrieve the newspaper. My crimes had made the lower left-hand corner of the front page of the *Times*: INNOCENT MAN SLAUGHTERS CELLMATE, the caption read. The article had my name and address, the details of the arrest with statements from the arresting officers, and an account of Lon Farthey's arrests and convictions.

I read the piece six times and then returned to my den to call Lena Clayborn.

"Just a moment and I'll connect you," a young man told me.

There was a short span of profound silence and then, "Lena speaking."

"You're in?" I said, somewhat surprised.

"Lawyers get paid by the pound," she replied. "Can you come in in an hour, Mr. Just?"

"Yes. I'll be there."

Celestine was sitting next to her mother, reading her book of magic realism. Tessa was asleep but looked to be on the verge of consciousness. She was restless even while at rest.

"You better get ready to go, honey," I said to my daughter.

"Can't I wait till she wakes up, Daddy?"

Brown was coming down the hall toward me. He was wearing black jeans and a dark-red T-shirt that had the words SMASH CUT printed in jagged letters across the chest in electric yellow.

"Wanna give me a ride to school, Dad?"

"Sure," I replied to both my children.

After dropping Brown off at the entrance of Hollywood High I drove downtown to a white stone office building on Grand. There, on the seventh floor, were the offices of Clayborn, Pettigrew, and Grey.

The skinny young Black man at the front desk knew me by sight. Somehow the people at the *Times* had found a photo of me at an office function, probably from an online site. He led me down a hall lined with bookshelves filled with law books and file folders, finally coming to a closed, cream-colored door.

He knocked.

"Come in."

The slender clerk pushed the door open, bidding me enter with the same gesture.

I walked into the sun-flooded room, surprised by the airiness and light.

I guess I looked impressed by Lena's digs because she said, "I get the morning sun. It makes me want to come to work early. How are you managing?"

"I feel like the best-known name in LA. Yesterday, it seemed like even my wife didn't know my name."

"Sit down, Mr. Just."

Clayborn's broad wooden desk was painted clamshell pink, while the two wooden chairs before it, looking very much like kitchen chairs, were a carefree turquoise.

"What are we going to do?" I asked my lawyer upon sitting.

"So you want me to represent you?"

"I thought we already settled that question."

"Your wife retained me, Mr. Just. I need you to accept her choice."

"Have you represented criminal cases before?"

"That's all I do. Tessa knew me because I represented an old boyfriend of hers—Truth Billings."

The mention of Truth sparked a question in my head.

"And what can you say about my problem?" I asked, pushing the speculation down.

"There's not much there to convict you on either charge. You were naked in public view . . ."

I suddenly had the almost irresistible urge to bite Ms. Clayborn. I was salivating and my jaws were clenched. Had I, in my sleep, been transformed into the living dead?

I closed my eyes and shivered.

"Is there something wrong, Mr. Just?"

"Call me Martin, will you, Lena? We, we shouldn't stand on ceremony."

I opened my eyes and forced a smile. Slowly, the impulse to devour my attorney ebbed away.

"As far as the manslaughter charge is concerned . . . Martin, the bruises on your throat trump the ones on your fists."

I sighed.

"It's all so crazy," I said.

"Do you remember what happened?"

"Only what I told the judge. I had that crazy dream and woke up disoriented. I'm still not right."

"I'd like you to go see my doctor. She can check you over for any underlying illness or trauma."

"Yeah," I said. "Okay. Maybe she'll be able to tell me something helpful."

An appointment was made by phone. Dr. Ella Portman would see me as soon as I could make it to her office on Wilshire Boulevard.

I stopped in the medical building's parking garage and called my wife.

"Hello?" Seal answered.

"You're still there, honey? I thought you were going to school."

"Mom needs me to hang around. And I really like this book."

"Is she up?"

"Mom," young Celestine called, and a moment passed.

In that small span of time I wondered what I could do to escape my feelings of doom. My parents were both dead. My mother had been an only child and my father an orphan. I had no brothers or sisters, first cousins, uncles, or aunts. There was no family for me to call. I didn't want Tessa or the children to have to bear my dread.

"Marty?" Tessa murmured. I had changed from her lover to husband once more. "How are you feeling, baby?"

"You haven't called me that in years."

"Time has fallen out of kilter," she said. I remember thinking that this was an odd choice of phrase.

"Where are you?"

"In a parking garage getting ready to go see a doctor."

"Is something wrong?"

"The lawyer sent me. How are you feeling?"

"The nausea is gone. But I'm seeing things."

"That doesn't sound good. Maybe you're the one who should go see a doctor."

"No," my wife said in a distant tone. "No. I'm not having hallucinations or anything like that. I'm *seeing* things that are very ordinary as if for the first time. I picked up the old thimble that came down from my great-great-grandmother, Narwyn. My mom told me that she used to be a seamstress on the Pinewood

Plantation in Hickton, Mississippi, over a hundred years ago.

"I studied the little finger cap for quarter of an hour. I saw the details and the way the finger pad was roughened to work against a needle's point. There's an enamel drawing of a white man in a top hat where the thumbnail fits. He's holding up a piece of cloth . . . I never noticed that before."

"What's wrong, baby?"

"Was that you with me last night?" Tessa asked.

"Of course it was me. You saw me, didn't you?"

"Yes. But you acted like another man. I called you Martin. I never call you Martin."

"I have to go to see this doctor, Tessa. Are you going to be all right?"

"I'm fine. I'm just keeping Seal around in case I get stuck looking at something."

"Stuck?"

"Go on, Marty. I'll see you when you get home."

"You can put your clothes back on, Mr. Just," Dr. Ella Portman said.

"Any bones broken in my hands?"

"No. Deep bruises, though. Were you in a fight?"

"I don't remember."

"There are no head injuries," she said, doubting my faulty memory.

Dr. Portman was over seventy, tall, and distinguished looking. She had silver hair and was quite thin. Her yellow eyes, behind gold-rimmed glasses, were deep set and inquisitive.

"I was in jail," I said. "That was the trauma."

"What were you arrested for?"

"Haven't you read the paper today?"

"I usually save all the papers up for Sunday and flip through them while on the exercise bike. Most of what you are told is lies. My father said that to me when I was just a child and I've always found it to be true."

"How am I, Doctor?"

"Are you a health enthusiast, Mr. Just?"

"No. I got three exercise machines sitting in the garage but never use them."

"Vegetarian?"

"If pork is eggplant and lobster tail is really a fruit of the sea."

"You have the skin and eyes of an infant and your muscle tone is impressive. You never exercise?"

"How's my blood?"

"We won't know that for a few days. But from everything I can tell, you are in excellent health for a man half your age."

I didn't go straight home. Instead I wandered over to Hancock Park and sat down on a bench next to the fenced-in tar pits. It was the most ancient place I knew of, and my mood was tending toward the prehistoric.

I couldn't, at the time, remember anything about the Plan other than that it was something as old as the ancestors of the atoms that my body was composed of. Beneath me, deep in the soil, lay the bones of wooly mammoths and saber-toothed tigers. This same history resided in my flesh, my bones. My existence was both impossible and eternally recurring, related to every event in the wide universe and particular, though in no way unique.

While I sat there watching the fence that kept the casual human or animal from meandering to its doom, I tried to understand my predicament.

Was I crazy? Maybe I'd had a stroke in the night. Dr. Portman hadn't used any advanced examination tools to scan my brain. My perception could have been off like a derailed high-speed train barreling through primordial woods.

It struck me that I had neither gone to work nor called to explain that I'd be out for a few days. The job I had worked at for seventeen years meant nothing to me.

Forty-seven. That's how old I was. Three and a half months and I'd be forty-eight. Tessa was ten years younger. She'd been going out with a drug dealer, the man named Truth Billings, when we, she and I, met at an upscale coffee shop in Westwood. I was working on my graduate thesis on ancient philosophy and she asked me why I was reading those boring books. I asked her out. She said that her boyfriend would kill me. Actually, she called him her old man. I took her to Santa Barbara for a three-day weekend. We talked and talked about school and the inherent opportunities connected to education. We didn't have sex. I felt impotent next to her vitality and beauty, but for some reason this caused her to have affection for me.

I took her home on Tuesday, and Truth was waiting inside. He was taller and blacker than I, with a vicious scar under his right eye. He pointed a pistol at my head and told me to get out.

I refused. This was the one act of true bravery in all of my forty-seven years.

Tessa told me to go.

Once again, I refused.

Truth told me that he would not hesitate to kill me.

I told him that I loved Tessa.

He said that she was his woman.

I asked him if he would die for her.

"Tessa?" he said.

"Yeah?" she replied.

"You love this niggah here?"

"I don't know for sure," she said, "but I think so."

He pressed the muzzle against my forehead.

"You know what I learned livin' in the street?" he asked.

"No."

"Whatever you can take from me—you can have."

He put the gun at the back of his pants, under a white gabardine jacket, and walked out of Tessa's studio apartment. They have remained friends over the years. He's been to prison and, Tessa tells me, is now out of the drug trade. I never see him. She's told me that he says he wants her back, but she tells him that she's got a family now and there's no going back from that.

Something about her claim seemed to have importance beyond our relationship, at least at that moment in time. There was no going back for me either. Whether I was crazy or something beyond Superman and his vaunted Fortress of Solitude, I could not go back to the man I was, living the meaningless if wonderful life of a mortal human being at the beginning of the twenty-first century.

The front door was open when I got home at 7:17 that evening. Normally, that simple fact would have scared me. I've always been a nervous kind of guy. But now an open door was just par for the course, as my father, a man who never golfed in his life, used to say.

"I'm home," I called upon entering the foyer of our modest two-story home.

"Here we are," a man said in a forced, coarse falsetto voice.

Three men in jeans, T-shirts, and tattooed white flesh met me in the living room. My family was seated on the long tan sofa. Brown's left eye was puffy and blackened, while Seal's jaw had a stoic set to it with contradictorily frightened eyes.

When Tessa's eyes met mine, they lit up and she gave a muted smile.

"It's the head nigger," the white man who had greeted me said. His voice was now a moderate tenor if still a bit coarse. "We been waitin' for you to start the party."

The other two men were standing guard behind my family.

It was all pathetically apparent. These men were associates of Lon Farthey. They had read, or had someone read to them, the address of my home in the irresponsible daily paper. I was to be tortured and killed but not before my wife and daughter were raped and my son slaughtered.

It was Temple who made these assumptions. I never would have jumped to conclusions so quickly. I was a thinker, a de facto diplomat. I would have asked what they wanted. Maybe I would have offered them money and my silence.

All Temple did was condemn and salivate. He hunched down like a dog in my breast. All I had to do was relinquish control and he would show me, and my grinning wife, what real manhood was.

I relaxed my hold on this physical realm and Temple leapt at the mouthpiece for the gang. With his/my left elbow he cracked the big, fat white man's jaw.

"Hey!" yelled both of his friends.

Then Temple socked the shocked leader right in the Adam's apple. His next action was a bit of a surprise. He bit viciously into the side of the man's neck.

I was, Temple was, leaping over the sofa while the defeated leader slumped to the floor. My inordinately powerful hands grabbed the closest and shortest man by the shoulders and slammed him against the wall with such force that he was immediately rendered unconscious. I bit into his jaw and let him drop.

When I turned to the last attacker, he was both afraid and armed with a vicious-looking hunting knife.

I quailed at the prospect, but Temple grinned.

"Get him, honey," Tessa said.

Time slowed to a quarter its natural speed. The last invader moved back, felt the wall behind him, and then came forward at a speed he believed was good enough to accomplish his murderous ends. I waited, waited, waited until the point of his blade was maybe four inches from my chest.

Celestine yelled.

I, or more correctly Temple, grabbed the big man's wrist, moved to the side while twisting the arm behind him, and then bit deeply into the back of his neck. He yelled and crumpled to the floor, disoriented and weak.

I used an ochre pillow from the sofa to wipe the blood from my lips and chin. I was still salivating, like a feral predator.

"Daddy!" Seal shouted, but it was Tessa who ran into my arms. She kissed my bloody mouth and grunted with secondhand satisfaction.

The real me, Marty, was appalled by my actions and her response. But Temple was in my hands and arms. It was Temple who returned her victorious kiss.

"Brown," Temple said.

"Yeah, Dad?"

"We're going to lay these guys out side by side on the floor here. Move the coffee table over against the wall."

The smaller guy was already unconscious so I moved him first. The other two were woozy, losing consciousness in slow motion. I pushed them down and laid them out on the floor next to their compatriot.

"Should I call the police?" asked Seal.

"No."

"Why not?"

"You'll see. Why don't you go in the kitchen and boil some water, honey?"

In a trance-like state, Celestine walked out of the living room. Tessa was holding my arm while Brown gazed vacantly, slowly giving in to shock.

"Get Brown a shot of whiskey," I said to my wife.

She grinned and left my side.

"Have a seat, son."

He backed toward the couch and fell rather than properly sitting down.

"I tried to stop them," he mumbled, "but that guy knocked me down."

He was pointing at the man I hit in the throat. I scanned the inert bodies. They were all unconscious. The first man I hit, the one who struck my son, might have been dead.

One by one I ripped open the fronts of their T-shirts. When I was finished Tessa returned with a water glass half filled with amber fluid. This she handed to our son.

"Drink as much as you can, Brown," I said. And then to my wife, "Go see about Seal."

Tessa smiled at me. She was a new woman, as changed as I was. I realized then, under the dominant worldview of Temple, that my *power* was to infect, with the edicts of infinity, my own blood. The men I fought were touched by the influence of my saliva, but in a more profound way Tessa was altered by the transmission of blood.

I went to the men one by one and laid my hand upon their bare chests. My palm felt hot.

The third man that I had bitten writhed in agony at the touch. Almost instantly I understood that he was responding to some kind of celestial contagion that manifested itself through the alpha personality that was now anchored to my mild and mortal being.

Brown sipped at his whiskey, not looking at the men laid out on the floor like dead and dying bodies set out in preparation for mass burial.

I waited.

Last bitten, first risen. The man who had only been infected by my saliva sat up and looked at me.

"What happened?" he asked.

"You and your friends came in here for retribution," Temple replied.

Sitting on his butt, hugging his knees, the man nodded.

"But all that's over now," I said, taking control from my newly minted alter ego.

Again the man nodded.

"What's your name?" I asked him.

"They call me Rat Man," the little guy said, nodding toward his unconscious cronies, "but my name is Mason, Mason Drinkman."

Looking into each other's eyes, Mason and I seemed to be transferring unconscious information. While we stared, my wife and daughter came in from the kitchen.

Brown was still sipping his whiskey.

The smaller man sat up.

His name was Sean Gardener, and he was also known as Reaper. He turned to a shivering Celestine and said, "I'm sorry for what we did and what we was gonna do. I don't even understand it now."

My daughter nodded and looked away. She would have fled if Tessa hadn't been holding her by the shoulders.

"What about Rooster?" Mason "Rat Man" Drinkman asked.

"He's dead," Temple said with my voice box.

Brown stood up suddenly, looking down on the corpse.

"You want us to take care of it?" Reaper asked.

"That won't be necessary," Temple replied.

And, as if responding to an implied command, the dead home invader sprang to life, coming to his feet and holding his deeply bruised Adam's apple. He began coughing, fell back onto his knees, and vomited thick, black fluid.

Wild-eyed, he said to the floor, "I was, was, was dead. I was dead."

Everyone in the room was staring at him, a little stunned. Even Temple was silent.

The would-be killer nicknamed Rooster looked up at the wall and said, "He's out there. He's out there." He was more afraid of the entity outside than he was of his own death and resurrection.

For a moment Temple and I shared the same point of view. There was someone outside—we could feel it too.

I moved toward the front of the house.

"Daddy!" Celestine protested.

"It's okay, Seal," Tessa assured her. "These men are no longer a danger to us."

I went out the front door and onto our well-manicured lawn. It was dark outside by then. Half a block away, equidistant between two lamp posts, successfully keeping himself to the shadows, stood a man of slender build. He wore a white trench coat and seemed to be bald, or maybe balding. I could feel him watching me, looking for some clue to my nature.

I could see why Resurrected Rooster was so disturbed. The man watching my house gave the impression of *hollowness*, a black hole that attracted and decimated all life. He was the Angel of Death.

I couldn't see his eyes but I could feel him watching me. In this way we became intimately aware of each other. I could feel his contempt for my beating heart and living mind. There was a moment of uncertainty. The man in the shadows was considering what action to take. Then Rat Man, Reaper, and Rooster came out on the lawn to join me.

They exuded prodigious health brought on by Temple's feral bites.

"That him?" Rat Man asked.

"He must have read about me in the papers too," I said, nodding.

"I don't think he can take all four of us," Rooster said. "But I won't be of much use against him."

"Yes," Temple agreed. "Because you were so recently dead, he will have some sovereignty over you."

"I'd resist him," Rooster told the man in my skin. "And you got these two and your wife. She's got some power, that one."

Maybe the man down the street could hear our words. He hunched his shoulders and then turned away. In a moment or two he was gone.

The five of us—three white-supremacist gangbangers, Temple, and I—stood for long minutes on the front lawn, stunned by the absence that the death-master's departure left in his wake. None of us, not even Rooster who died and was resurrected, had ever been in the presence of anything so absolute, so crushing.

There was no longer any doubt in my mind that I had been altered in the Long Sleep of Transformation. All of us, five men in four bodies, stood in that terrible moment of grace. We were all out of our depth like shipwrecked sailors afloat on a calm sea rife with sleek, brown-tipped sharks.

And there was blood in the water.

Tessa was in the kitchen making hot chocolate when we came back into the house. Brown was slouched over on the couch and Seal had gone up to her room.

The home invaders with their torn T-shirts and new outlooks took seats around my son while I went to visit with my wife. I wasn't worried about Brown's safety, because we were all on one side—at least for the moment.

Tessa watched me while chopping the block of unsweetened chocolate she used for this special treat.

"Is he gone?" she asked.

"The man outside?"

"The other one," she said. "The one in you."

"Yes," I said, a little surprised by the revelation that Temple was not omnipresent in my consciousness.

"I couldn't see him until after the fever was gone," she said. "But I could tell when you—when he—started fighting."

"I don't know what I think about that," I said. "About him."

"He's just a part of you," my wife comforted. "Something that was created out of necessity. That was you making love to me."

"It didn't feel like it."

"No," she agreed, "but I can see that he comes out of the long road of your mind."

"Why can't I see that? It's like, it's like I forgot everything."

"You are the fount, Marty," Tessa told me. "You cannot be aware. But I can read you because we have the same blood. And those men out there, they receive something too—something that gives them purpose beyond revenge. We all know our missions, but you, and the man inside you, act on reflex and instinct."

"Why?"

"Because that's the way it is."

While talking, Tessa warmed the milk and blended in the fancy chocolate and brown sugar. She put some white powder in a red mug, two shots of brandy in a blue one, and then poured the hot confection into five white cups and the two mugs.

"Hot chocolate!" she cried.

I brought the men, including my son, in from the living room while Tessa collected our frightened daughter from her upstairs bedroom.

Once we were all gathered around the high table in the kitchen, Tessa gave the red mug to our daughter and the blue one to our son. The rest of us grabbed the white cups and drank.

"My mother used to make hot chocolate," Reaper said. "She used powder out of a can that already had sugar in it, but me and Malcolm loved that stuff, man. She'd only do it when we had both been good for a few days, so it was only about once a month or so that we got it, but it was extra sweet because of that."

After finishing his little speech, Reaper—Sean Gardener—went quiet, reflecting on a long life. I thought that he might be wondering about the chocolate he was drinking right then—how that particular brew was a portent for what might come.

"Only chocolate milk I ever had was cold," Rooster said. He had a wide, florid face with gray eyes and two missing teeth. His voice was rough and hoarse, ingratiating in a roguish way. "Mama used to buy a box of sweet powder and a gallon of milk. They'd both be gone by morning."

"Drink your chocolate," Tessa said to Celestine.

Our frightened daughter obeyed.

"What happened to us?" Rat Man asked me.

I waited for a beat to see if Temple would come out and answer.

When he didn't respond, I said, "I had a dream."

"A dream?" Rooster rasped. "What kinda dream?"

"I don't remember it completely," I said. "As a matter of fact, I don't remember very much. There was a declaration in the farthest reaches of infinity that life here on Earth threatened the well-being of existence."

"The universe is afraid of a little man?" Rooster said quizzically.

"Not just humanity," I said, speaking a truth that I was not quite aware of. "Life itself, the DNA molecule, is the threat, along with the machinations and machines that we produce."

"But only men make machines," Reaper said.

"The only real machine is the molecule we're made from," I replied. "One day we will splice ourselves with lions and porcupines, sharks and larks. We will build machines attached to our neurons, and each of us will grow to proportions greater than this solar system. The sad truth is that because we can imagine the universe, we can also destroy it."

Celestine shivered and then yawned.

Brown's head was drooping and I worried that he might fall off his high stool.

"You kiddin', right?" Rat Man said in response to my obviously exaggerated claim.

"Not at all. We are an anomaly, an infection."

"Like you get with strep throat or the clap?" Reaper asked.

Rooster nodded, agreeing with the underlying meaning of the question.

"Yes," I said.

"But don't an infection need a body to live on?" Rooster said.

"The universe is a living thing—actually an inter-dependent collection of living things that coexist and have done so through a billion trillion reiterations."

"I don't get ya," Rat Man said. In one way or another all three men were reborn, but that didn't increase their vocabularies.

"The universe is a phoenix," I explained, wondering what Temple would think of my words. "It dies in flame and is reborn from the ashes again and again, every time the same but . . . deeper, more complex. DNA-based life is but one of these added complexities."

"And what's our job?" Reaper asked.

Seal fell from her stool but Resurrected Rooster was there to catch her.

"Her bedroom is the first one on the left at the top of the stairs," Tessa said to a man who just an hour before was her mortal enemy.

"Our job is to save life, or as much of it as possible, from the insanity of the Eschaton," I said as the portly racist carried my daughter from the room.

"Say what?" Reaper asked.

"There is a delicate dance done by all the matter, antimatter, gravities, temporal incongruities, and less explainable forces of the universe. Before the beginning there was mostly nothing and nowhere. Somehow the beings that now form our universe willed themselves into existence. If life has its way, that delicate balance will be dissolved and all that ever was, the same and not the same, will be as if it had never been.

"Like a man when he dies," Rooster said.

The big thug had returned from my daughter's bedroom. He had a very serious look in his gray eyes.

"But on a much grander scale," I said.

"A man is bigger than a ant," Rooster argued. "A ant is even bigger compared to a germ. But they all die. They all face this—what you call it—this dissolving."

"What are you getting at?" I asked the tattooed behemoth.

"I died and came back to life," he said. "There's something wrong with that. It's like goin' to bed on a Thursday and wakin' up the Tuesday before."

Temple smiled with my mouth and said, "I don't give a fuck about what the cosmic forces want or don't want. I'm here to make sure that your babies have babies and that the forests can grow in ignorant bliss. I'm here so that guy we saw outside, and a dozen more like him, don't get their way and just wipe out all life."

"And who are you?" Rat Man asked.

"What?" Brown said to this question. He got off the counter stool and staggered on his feet toward Mason Drinkman. Rat Man wasn't small, but his taupe hair was naturally spikey and he had eyebrows arched up in rodent-like fashion.

"That's my father," Brown slurred. He was drunk and confused. I think he was intending to throw a punch.

But Tessa put her arms around him and he wobbled to a standstill.

"Come upstairs with me, BB," she said.

"But he said that about Pops," Brown complained.

"Come on," she said, pulling on his brawny, footballer arms.

They staggered toward the hall and stairway.

My template turned to Rat Man and said, "I am the Martin Just that Martin Just always wanted to be. I'm strong and fast and believe what I think to be the right way to do things. He calls me Temple. You can too if you want."

"There's a whole lotta people out there like that man we saw in the street?" asked Reaper.

"About a dozen."

"It woulda been touch and go with all of us up against him alone. Don't ask me how, but I could feel the power comin' offa him."

"Yeah, but, there's more out there like me, too," Temple replied. "And there's others who have jobs that I can't even explain."

"How many?" Rooster asked.

"One hundred and six, seven if you include me."

"And they're all out there wanting to end all life?" Rat Man asked.

"Marty wants to save the world. Dead Man out there wants to end it. Some of us are interested in trees or fish—or the planet itself, which will almost certainly survive the writhing molecule. It's our job to resolve our differences."

"What does that mean?" Rooster asked.

"Either kiss, kill, or isolate."

The three white men in torn white T-shirts stared at Temple, wondering what to ask next. But before they could bring another question to a level of articulation, Temple said, "You guys should clear out of here for the night. The kids are still scared of you and Marty needs some time with his wife."

"Suppose we say no?" Rooster challenged. This was the first indication that the change had not made him a vassal as I had at first supposed.

"I'll kill you," Temple said.

"You think you could take all three of us?"

"I did once already tonight."

"Come on, Harold," Reaper said to Rooster. "We done messed with these people enough already."

A few beats went by while the man who sometimes inhabited my body and the men who had been intent on slaughtering my family faced off.

"When you want us to come back?" Rat Man asked at last.

"At the end of the day tomorrow," Temple said, "after five. And when you're out there, look out for that pale guy. Don't think you can take him. You can't, and we can't lose you guys. Not yet."

Temple walked the three members of the Aryan gang to the door. As he watched them leave, his resolve dissipated and I became myself again.

It was an odd feeling—like having a blockage pulled out of your nasal cavity. It felt good and at the same time somehow uncomfortable.

I stood there for long minutes, at the open front door. The dark block had not changed but the universe had placed its full attention there. It was an invisible, intangible miracle—an event I would have preferred never to have been aware of.

"Marty?" Tessa was standing there behind me.

"You can tell the difference between us?"

"I can," she admitted, "but it's hard to say how. But both men are you, baby. One of them is just free of his, his inhibitions."

"And he can fuck you while standing up and beat two men twice his size to death in the span of half a day. Then he can raise one of those men from the dead."

"He had sex with me to pass on your blood," she said, as if I weren't expressing my rage. "I can see that there's a full-fledged war being waged by a hundred and seven warriors. You're one of those warriors. The man you're so jealous of is just another aspect of you."

"But it's like I'm just a butler or a janitor and all you—Rooster, Temple, and all the rest—are more aware, more powerful . . . more important."

Tessa smiled at me and shook her head lovingly. She said, "You're like the king in a chess game. Your survival is our only hope."

"Why the fuck is he so much stronger than me?"

"I keep telling you, baby, he is you."

That conversation might have gone on for hours. We could have said the exact same words over and over again, mimicking the recurring universe that had tasked me and my brethren with changing everything.

We could have talked forever but Tessa said, "We have to go upstairs."

"What for?"

She turned away and walked into the house. I resisted going after her for three long minutes. I wanted the trajectory of the world, seemingly set in motion by my dream, to stop. I thought that if I could just stay still, the danger would pass.

But standing there in the dark, moonless night, I knew that there was no escape from this unasked for destiny. Even my own mind was given over to the task of saving a doomed world.

I went into the electric glare of the silent house and walked up the stairs, more like a man sentenced to death than an interstellar agent set against the absolute holocaust posed by all things living.

There were two single beds set against opposite walls in Celestine's room. She had asked for the pair of smaller beds in lieu of a larger one because she often had friends sleep over and this was a good way to accommodate her social tendencies. Seal was unconscious on her side and Brown was out cold on the visitor's cot.

On a small table that Tessa had dragged between the two beds was her old medical bag from when she did a stint as a nurse for Doctors without Borders. I had convinced her to take this job after she got her nursing degree. When she returned, she told me that she loved me because my passion for her set her free rather than limiting her to what everyone else expected.

Next to the table was a pink padded chair that Seal used to sit in front of her blue vanity.

Tessa gestured at the chair and I sat obediently.

From the bag she took out two sealed packages containing single-use hypodermics. As she severed the packages with a scalpel, Tessa spoke.

"You saved my life, Marty," she said. "I know I always let you think that I was happy to get with a man that I could throw around in the bed, that I could make him feel like there was no coming down. But none of that was true . . ." She took out the first injection device and looked at me. "You risked your life to take me away, and all you did was tell me how

80

much you were learning. It was on that holiday I knew that I could be somebody and not somebody's dog."

She reached into the bag and took out a small bottle of liquid and a cotton ball.

"Roll up your left sleeve, baby," she said, "and swab down the skin just above the crook of the arm."

"Why did Seal faint?" I asked while doing what I was told.

"I crushed three sleeping pills and put them in her cocoa."

"Why?"

She grasped my forearm and expertly drew the blood. Then she went over to Celestine's bed and injected her in the hip. My daughter's lips parted and her eyes opened. She looked right at me but I don't think she saw anything.

"Once more," my wife said.

She approached me with the second needle and I held out a hand to stop her.

"What?" she asked.

"We haven't discussed this," I said. "We always talk about things, Tess. That's something we agreed on way back in the beginning."

"Words are what humans use because they have lost or maybe they never had the talent for knowing," she said. This phrase seemed familiar but I couldn't remember where it had come from. "You gave me your blood, baby. Everything is in that. The dogs have been loosed on the world and you might be the only one who can save us—leaf and fin, scale and mind."

"But I don't remember."

"Give me your right arm."

She took more blood and then said, "Hold Brown down while I inject him."

The request alone called up Temple. He moved through my skin to hold Brown by the shoulders. When the high school quarterback bucked from the pain, my inner anchor held him down with ease. A moment after the inoculation Brown fell back into restful unconsciousness.

I stared at my son, wondering how I could be involved in such perversions without even a discussion. He was my boy and I loved him without expectation. He could have been anything, done anything, and I would still adore him. But I was proud of him too. He'd fought with the big Aryan avenger. He had suffered for not being strong enough to protect his mother and sister.

I felt something wet and soft against the webbing of skin between my left thumb and forefinger. Looking, I saw that Tessa had knelt down to kiss that hand.

Temple, who had not strayed far from my consciousness, lifted her in my arms and took her to the bedroom.

I had never brought such cries of pleasure from my wife. She writhed and whispered, scratched bloody welts across my back, and whenever I came, she froze as if in some kind of religious trance.

It was a grueling experience. Temple and Tessa were ecstatic, but I felt like the third wheel on a unicycle. At one point in the middle of their rapture Temple asked, "Have you been having sex with that man Truth?"

A look of terror appeared on her face. She grabbed me by the head and said, "Never again, baby. I promise you that."

That was when I realized that Temple was indeed a part of me. His rage at Tessa's infidelity drove him to such an extreme level of violence that he exited my body in mid-stroke, leaving me shaken and confused.

"Marty?" my blood-wisened wife said.

"You've been sleeping with him?" I asked.

"We'd been together since I was in my early teens. It was him that I looked up to before you . . . and now you."

I sat down in half lotus at the end of the bed. Temple's erection was now my limp cock. His rage was my philosophical attempt to make sense of betrayal. Maybe that's why the forces of existence homed in on me. I was a wise man and therefore their fool. We philosophers ask questions because we sit on the outside of being, imagining that thought somehow has influence over reality.

"I never satisfied you?" I said.

"You gave me everything, Marty."

"You call him Martin."

"I'm sorry. I was raised in a place where men had to be violent and tough-minded. But I needed you. I need you more than Martin or Truth."

"Except with sex," I said. "Except when you need to be with a man."

Tessa looked at me. I could see her pain reflecting my humiliation. I could see how much she loved me and needed me and, at the same time, how she'd never gotten past the perceived needs of her so-called disadvantaged past.

We were both Black people, she and I, but race doesn't come with a manual and a code of behavior—only our genes do that.

I shook my head and got up off the bed.

"Where are you going?" Tessa asked.

"Do you love him?"

"Which one?"

"The blood," I said then. "Is it like a conduit between what I dreamed and what you know?"

"How I see things and just a few ideas," she said, "like the hundred and seven."

"Were you ever just with me?"

"I started seeing Truth when he got out of prison, seven years ago. He was so broken and scared. He saved me from a bad situation when I was a child."

"So Brown and Seal are mine?"

"Of course. Of course they are."

"Which one?"

"I just told you. Both children are yours."

"Which man do you love?"

"I'm your wife, Marty. In my heart I am only yours."

"Okay then. To answer your question, I'm going downstairs."

Free will is the fount of all unhappiness. That's what my professor back at university, Dondi Muller, used to say. He was from Copenhagen and bisexual. He lived in a three-bedroom flat with his daughter Igga and an old man named Furman.

Planets don't mind the fiery pain of birth or the inevitable crush of existence, he'd say. *Beams of light do not question the arc of their passage. Only life defies fate. Only life tries to alter the course of rivers and the pull of gravity . . .*

Sitting on the long couch in my living room, I remembered the lecture for the first time since it was given. That was at a brown bag lunch-talk that a young undergrad named Tiffany Lumpkin wanted to attend. I thought that if I brought her she'd agree to go out with me, but Tiffany and Muller hooked up three days after that brown bag lunch-talk.

He had been my advisor but I dropped him over the Tiffany thing.

And now his words came back to counsel me about my role as an antibody in the loosely connected body of life on Earth.

. . . *but neither can the stuff of existence know happiness*, Professor Muller had said. *Rocks don't cuddle or giggle, nor do they feel awe at the dawning of the day. Life imbues matter with meaning and this, this small and intangible projection, creates the space that we call the soul.*

I wondered if my bite worked differently than a direct blood injection. I almost went upstairs to ask Tessa but the door to our communications was closed—at least for the moment.

Could my blood affect animals? Could Tessa or Rooster infect others as I had?

Should I kill myself? Would that stop the seemingly inert matter of the universe from committing genocide on all life?

This line of thought led to the real question that plagued me back when the world had not yet begun to change—back before the rise of the Eternal City and the March of Death. That question was: *Am I crazy?*

I looked around the room where I had murdered a man and brought him back to life before the last breath fled his body.

Maybe I belonged in an institution.

It occurred to me that if I allowed professionals to examine my body and mind, they could say whether I seemed competent or not. They could identify schizophrenia or psychosis in my behavior or abnormalities in my blood. Maybe this was why my delusions tended toward concepts of the blood. Or maybe, maybe Tessa and I had experienced one of those rare mental disorders in which we labored under the same or similar delusions.

There came a loud chime from the front door.

This was odd because our doorbell was a distinctly unmusical buzzer.

I waited a moment to see if Tessa would come running down—but she didn't.

So I went to the door and opened it.

Standing there in the glare of the porch lamp was the slender man in the white trench coat. He was bald and his eyes were the color of liquid mercury.

His pallid skin seemed almost synthetic. There was such stillness in his mien that it felt to me as if time had ceased or, at least, had paused in the space he inhabited.

"Our souls once mingled," he said.

"Who are you?"

"You are the one that was known as the Antibody and the Cure." The little dome-headed white man sneered, evoking disdain and dismissal with the expression.

Temple tried to take over my body but I, somehow, stopped him. While I was concentrating on suppression, the waxy white man reached out and grabbed my left wrist. Where he held me I felt a ring of cold. This was not an inert sensation but like a living organism attempting to worm its icy way through my flesh.

I gasped at the feeling. It was like I had stuck my hand in the freezer and had been lassoed by the coils of a snake made of ice.

The small man smiled.

A shiver went down the back of my neck and made its way down my left arm to the place where the living cold had entered. The little white man looked up in mild surprise and then his hand leapt from my wrist like a cold frog from a heated stone.

My temperature rose, fever-like. My breath became shallow and fast.

Somewhere Temple was straining against an impassable barrier.

I smiled at my ability to resist both the white man and the man inside me.

"My name is Tor Waxman," the bald man said in a conciliatory tone. "May I come in for a few moments?"

"Why?"

"We are brothers," he said simply.

If he had said anything else, threat or compliment, I would have turned him away. But his assertion of our kinship was like the evocation of an unbreakable bond. Whether we liked each other or not, whether we were enemies or not, we were still bound.

His claim of affinity proved to me that I was not insane. He was really there, standing before me—not a hallucination but some kind of omnipotent angel loosed upon mortality like a magnificent and hungry tiger set on a field of grazing sheep.

I stood aside and gestured for him to enter. He went into the living room and sat upon a wooden chair painted yellow by my wife during the first year of our marriage.

Perching on the edge of our couch I asked, "So you went to sleep and woke up transformed?"

"I died three days ago," he said. "But before the last figments of life passed from my brain I was drawn into the Beyond by the forces that also took you."

"Like an alien abduction?"

"That idea is so human," Tor Waxman said, curling the left side of his upper lip. "We were the focus of the gods, the very stuff of the universe. You and I are harbingers of the Divine."

"And what message is it that you believe we are here to deliver?" I asked.

"Death to life."

"You're kidding."

"The sham of life represents a cancer on the natural order of being, Martin Just."

"How do you know my name?"

"I might be dead," Waxman said. "I might be a demon but I can still read the newspaper. I died up in Riverside and awoke next to a woman the man I had been was married to for twenty years. As I took her life, I felt you. That afternoon I arrived in LA. The next morning I knew that it was you in the papers."

"You murdered your wife?"

"I returned her to the Infinite."

"And what do you want to do with me?"

"Between the effects of your bodily fluids and the effects of my touch we can raise an army of the obedient dead. Through these dead and deathless soldiers we can begin the eradication of all life."

I stared into his silver eyes. Waxman did not blink.

"Why?"

"You know why."

"But life is precious."

"The idea of self-importance is an illusion. Life is stupid. Only eternity is precious."

Temple was at the back of my mind, ranting to be released. He wanted to go to war with Waxman.

I remained calm and by doing so kept him at bay.

"No," I said. "I cannot be a part of absolute genocide."

"There is no other way."

"If that's so, why not just make Mars go out of orbit and crash into us?" I said. "Or maybe urge the sun to go supernova and burn life away? If this is God we're talking about, why fool around with insignificant beings like you and me?"

"You really don't know the answer to those questions?" he asked.

"No."

"Eternity is quiescent. Aware in a way that only absolute being can be. It is not a physical thing, not at the root. Matter is simply the outline of a greater being."

"But I met many different beings in my sleep."

"All aspects of one master force, as you and I are parts of a single plan."

"If the universe is dormant, then how did it take you and me and all those others?" I asked. "How were we transformed?"

"In the moment of what the science of this species calls the big bang, there is a nanosecond of motive for Being. During this transition, in the last bout of existence, the potential threat of life made itself manifest. When the current big bang occurred, in that brief tick of intention, a message was sent to the appropriate agents and we were created."

"You're saying that the experience I had, we had, was crafted billions of years ago?"

"Sixty-two oh five six three nine one eight eight nine zero zero zero one five two six seven so-called years past." Tor Waxman smiled at the utterance of this number as if it were sacred.

"If we both come from the same place, why can't I remember all this?"

"That is the right question," he said through a deathly grin. "My . . . situation, my being dead made me more like the masters. I remember almost everything . . . almost."

"You remember that we are supposed to raise this army of the dead?"

"It's only logical."

"What is this, this touch—your power?" I asked then.

"Death," he said. "Any life-form I touch will die within twenty-four to one hundred and sixty-eight hours."

"But not me." Somehow I knew this was true. "You knew that, but you had to try to kill me anyway."

"I didn't know for sure."

"So you don't know everything."

"Marty," Tessa said. She had entered the room from the doorway that led to the stairs.

Waxman leapt to his feet and ran at her. He grabbed her by both wrists.

"Oh!"

There was a moment when time stood still. Tor Waxman raised Tessa's arms high as in triumph. I knew exactly what was transpiring. Soon, at the end of the day or, at most, the week, my wife would die from the dead man's touch. The only way to save her was by my blood or spittle. And then she would transform into some kind of New Age zombie answerable to Waxman, intent on devastation.

I hated him then.

Tessa's eyes closed and then opened. They were completely white, with neither pupil nor iris. Her mouth went slack and it seemed as if she'd fall. But then she closed her eyes and opened them again. Everything was normal and she brought down her arms with a triumphant whoop. Tor Waxman fell away from her and cowered.

Tessa caressed her wrists with either hand and I found the strength to stand.

"You have shielded them," Waxman said to me.

Tessa stumbled to the yellow chair and sat.

"You're smarter than you pretend to be, Anti-body," the embodiment of death rasped.

Temple was clawing at my resistance while Tessa sobbed on her chair.

Suddenly Waxman stood upright, a hunting knife in his left hand.

"But she can still die the pedestrian death," he said.

Temple came forth in me like a madman ripping out of a straitjacket.

Waxman's silver eyes widened and without pre-amble he turned and ran.

I was satisfied to let him go but Temple was not of the same opinion—and he was in charge.

Death is fleet.

He ran down the center line of Charbadon Lane, the street we lived on. I barreled after him with the grim determination of a predator, of another man who controlled my body.

Tor cut down an alley, jumped on top of a parked car, and leapt from there to the roof of the garage.

To my surprise I was able to match him step for leap.

He hopped into the backyard behind the home we skipped over, ran across another driveway and then off into the Hollywood Hills.

I followed close behind.

The ground was uneven and the vegetation made the run an obstacle course, but Death was not stymied and neither was I.

All around me I perceived the souls of living things. They quailed at the passage of Death. And I kept running, driven by the intensity of my alter ego, my adolescent ideal of a perfect self.

Through more private properties, down a series of blacktop streets, and onto Hollywood Boulevard we ran. The boulevard was crowded with cars and pedestrians. Waxman was half a block ahead of us. We were slowly closing that gap when he stopped at a pink Cadillac. He opened the driver's-side door and pulled the man sitting there out and onto the sidewalk. He jumped behind the wheel and without closing the door he hit the gas, running up on the curb, plowing through a crowd of pedestrians.

Temple moved to copy Death's actions. He took a step toward a copper-colored Buick but I clinched down on him. We froze in mid-step. I was the cage and

Temple the trapped beast. I could feel him straining against my will but I would not relent. Tor Waxman didn't care about innocent life, neither did Temple.

There were shouts and screams, moans from the injured, and many, many bodies that littered the street and sidewalks. I was breathing harder than I ever had before. My lungs sucked down air desperately. I put my hands on my knees.

Nobody noticed me because they were all running toward, or away from, the carnage that Waxman had wrought.

I couldn't get enough air.

People were screaming.

Within a minute or two, sirens sounded.

With great concentration I stood upright. And, while the street wailed and cried, I staggered back the way I had come.

The walk back home was the coda of one life and the beginning of another. I lurched, stiff-legged, up the hillside on a path Brown and I had often used on our walks together. I felt like a soldier from some long-ago war, walking home after a mighty conflagration in which all the foot soldiers on both sides of the battle had lost more than they'd gained. In the distance I could hear the mechanical wails of a dozen or more ambulances. I was still breathing hard.

Temple had taken my body to the extreme of its endurance. He was the warrior, where I was just a draftee hoping to survive, traumatized by the ugliness of war.

Halfway up the trail a huge bright-green moth with long, elegant gossamer wings landed on my left shoulder. I didn't brush it away.

Together, the moth and I climbed the Hollywood Hills. We reached the path that led to the web of small lanes that brought us finally to Charbadon.

The door to my home was open again. It had been left that way from the frantic chase after Waxman.

Tessa was still sitting on the yellow chair that she had painted so long ago. She was caressing her wrists and staring off into space when I knelt before her and put my head on her lap.

We didn't speak for a long time.

And then there came a soft, beautiful humming sound. It was a complex interweaving of melodies that were both otherworldly and distinctly alive. Inside the composition were supernovas and peasant dances, tin horns and pure vibrations that moved between the folds of space.

"Where did you find it?" Tessa asked.

Taking in a deep breath, the final gulp I needed for recuperation, I saw that the great moth had moved from my shoulder to her hands and wrists. The music emanated from the emerald insect.

"It found me," I said.

"Is he dead?"

"He escaped. He jumped in a car and ran down a crowded block of people. The man you call Martin wanted to follow but I wouldn't let him."

"Let's go to bed," she said.

We slept in Celestine's room, me with Brown and Tessa with our daughter. The moth draped its nine-inch-long wings down the lamp on the desk. It purred a strain that led inward and downward, across a plain of stars and darkness.

"Dad."

Someone was shaking me.

"Dad."

I opened my eyes to Brown's burly shoulders and brooding mien.

The moth had arranged itself on the window. The transparent wings seemed to glitter in the sunlight.

The other bed across the room was empty.

"Where's your mother and sister?"

"Downstairs." Brown's eyes peered into mine. We were seeing things in each other that we'd not known a few days before. We were kin and kindred but there was more. Our family had increased to include all life. And life itself had become a solitary entity writhing in its own skin—becoming.

I sat up with some effort.

"The phone's for you," Brown said. "It's after twelve."

Phones and clocks didn't seem the appropriate topic. We should have been discussing the pulse of existence and what the past had rendered unto the present.

"It's your lawyer," Brown said as if in counterpoint to my thoughts. "Mom says that you have to talk to her."

My son held out his hand. I snagged it and he pulled me up and out of bed with ease. I was wearing black slacks and a white T-shirt, no shoes or socks.

I closed my eyes and opened them.

"How do you feel, son?"

"Like I could walk up into the sky and disappear."

We embraced and I went downstairs, wondering if I was the disease and not the cure.

"Hello?" I said into the phone in my den.

"I expected to hear from you before now, Mr. Just."

Just—yes, that was my name.

"I don't remember you asking me to call."

"Mr. Just, you can't take this thing lightly. The prosecutor wants your head."

"I assure you, Ms. Clayborn, that I am not treating these accusations superficially. It's just that I've been trying to come to grips with the ramifications in my life. I was so upset and exhausted that I only just woke up when you called."

"Then you need an alarm, Mr. Just."

"Did you hear from the doctor?"

"She said that you were fine except for the bruises on your throat and hands. The trauma to your neck, she said, definitely came from an attempt to strangle you."

"That's good, right?" I said.

"Nothing's one hundred percent with Fyodor Trapas against you."

"I'm sorry if I seem flip or uninvolved or anything, Ms. Clayborn. Is there something I can do now?"

The buzzer for the front door sounded at that moment. This reminded me of the chime that went off in my mind when Tor Waxman called. As I thought of Waxman, a thrill of fear for the safety of my family went through me.

I was still worried about something so insignificant as a single family unit; an infinitesimal piece of one of a billion trillion beings that comprised existence.

"I guess not," Lena Clayborn was saying in my ear. "Excuse me for chastising you, Mr. Just. I'm only trying to make sure that you get the best representation."

"It's the police, Dad," my daughter said at the door of the den.

"Thank you, Ms. Clayborn. I might be calling you soon."

Two uniformed members of the LAPD stood at my front door. They were talking to my wife.

". . . no, no," Tessa was saying. "I mean, I did hear the sirens last night but I haven't listened to the radio or watched TV this morning."

The policemen were both white, both male. They were young. One was pudgy and the other thin. They were living beings: revolutionary insurgents, by definition, against the quiescent universe.

"Hello," I said.

The great green moth floated down the stairs, landing on the wall above the front door. One of the cops, the heavyset one, looked up to see where it had gone.

"Mr. Just?" the thin cop said.

"Yes."

"There was a crime committed down on Hollywood Boulevard last night. A crazy man, maybe under the influence of drugs, hijacked a car and drove it down a crowded sidewalk."

"Oh no," Temple said. "Was anyone seriously hurt?"

"There have been nineteen fatalities so far. A few of the thirty-nine people in the hospital are critical."

"My God," Temple blasphemed. "Do you think that the man is from up around here?"

The chubby policeman looked down from the moth and into my eyes.

"Why would you ask that?" he asked.

"Because you're here telling me about the crime," my template proclaimed. "I doubt that you'd be wasting your time for any other reason."

"A few witnesses said that they saw a Black man chasing the carjacker," the heavy cop stated. "They were both running pretty hard."

Brown moved to my side, catching the skinny policeman's attention.

"I didn't see anything like a chase. Was the car-jacker a Black man too?"

"No."

I was of two minds—literally. Temple wanted to grab the police and bite them. He wanted to make sure that we didn't have any further complications with the law.

I, on the other hand, did not believe that there was any concrete evidence against me and wanted to let the scene play out until the officers left.

I won.

The policemen were suspicious. We were the only Black family on the block and one of the few in the hills. But there was no justification to arrest any of us.

The chubby cop gave me his card. It read, "Officer Clement Riley," with an email address and phone number at the Hollywood precinct.

After the policemen left I closed the front door. Tessa, Brown, and I stood in the small foyer as if waiting for something. The green moth began to hum.

It was almost mechanical, the dirge. It gave me the feeling of being inside a great motor that was idling.

"What are you guys doing?" Seal asked from the top of the stairs.

She skipped down to us, smiling and carefree.

"Just . . . um," Brown said. "Just hanging around."

"What's your problem?" she asked. "You're acting like something terrible happened when really it's both—terrible and wonderful too. Can't you feel it?"

"What?" I asked.

"Everything," she said. "The sun and the trees and even the ground. It's like we were living in a dark hole all this time and now we've been unearthed. We can see."

The moth's tune brightened, seemingly in reaction to my daughter's words.

"But all those people . . ." I said.

"Who died," Seal finished the sentence. "I know. Mom told me. We have to stop him. We have to keep him from killing everyone."

"Yeah," Brown said. "We have to, have to stop him."

Tessa held up her head and smiled.

I realized that there was a grin on my lips.

At that moment we were closer than we had ever been. Our blood was tuned by the moth over the door. But, as close as we were, we each had our own particular bent, our callings. From my nearly impotent schizophrenia to Celestine's irrepressible optimism and certainty, we were a unit devised for . . . something.

"I'm hungry," Brown said.

"Let's go for pizza," Tessa, my adulterous wife, offered.

Rufio's Pizza Paradise on Melrose was a favorite of the children. We took a back booth that was fairly secluded from the rest of the seating.

The only way I can describe the meal with my family after the annunciation of my destiny is to say that it was like an experience I had when I was a teenager living down the hill. My parents had moved from Massachusetts to LA because my mother had gotten a job teaching literature at USC.

Back then my girlfriend, Debbie Swanson, made brownies laced with a good deal of golden hashish.

She and I and two friends from school ate the whole pan and then went walking down the beach. After an hour or so I realized that we were all talking and looking around, hearing snatches of what each other said and luxuriating in the wind and sand and sea.

"Hey, guys," I remember saying, "do you see what we're doing?"

We stopped and looked around in wonder, paused there appreciating that moment of grace. After a minute or two we started walking and talking again.

"We're still doing it," Debbie said.

Again we stopped and marveled.

Again we moved on, babbling and reveling in the pleasure.

"It was as if I had died," Tessa was saying. "He took hold of my wrists and ice shot up my arms. I was, was engulfed by cold and emptiness. It wasn't only that I was dead but it was as if I had never been alive. Somehow he had undone everything I stood for—my parents and children and those times when I was so happy I could hardly hold it in.

"And then, just when my eyes could no longer see, there was this red shimmering in the distance. It was like a sunrise over the entire universe. Everything was bright and all distances were relative. I could see it all and it all made sense—even that man Waxman. He brought me to that higher awareness and made it possible for me to throw him off . . ."

"I was on a football field," Brown recalled. I noticed as he spoke that he'd been growing larger, more well-defined. "And instead of two teams it was just me running up against all these animals. There was a boar and a rhinoceros, a pack of hyenas, and this big albino tiger pacing back and forth at the goal line. And I was running with the ball and the goal was a thousand miles away. Every kind of beast was running after me and at me but I kept on going.

"And the strangest thing was, when I would jump over some dog or alligator, when I was in the air, it felt like, like forever. When I jumped, time would stop and I could see everything in front and behind. I had all the time in the world to plan my strategy. I could see my opponents and I knew that if I didn't let fear take over, I could make it all the way to that white tiger, and maybe even score."

"There was that moth on the lamp and she sang to me," Celestine said. "They were real words but not in English or any human language. It was a story about moths and spiders and moonlight that shone so brightly that you had to go crazy and it was okay because things don't make sense anyway.

"Then I climbed up out of my body and when I looked down I saw Brown running and Mama naked with a sword and shield. Daddy had two faces and he was looking from side to side. Then he stood up and was just one man and he came to me. He kissed my forehead and asked if this was the right thing and I told him that there were two things, that there were always two things. Daddy asked what were they, and I said that it was what was behind and what was ahead. And when I said that, I knew that it was from the moth's song, I knew it and kissed Daddy on the lips."

111

*   *   *

I don't remember talking at the pizza restaurant. I think I must have said something profound but the ideas were to be shared, not hoarded.

We ate seven large pizzas with every topping except pineapple and anchovies. I was in a daze and reveling in the beauty of my family.

"How did you know to inject us with Dad's blood?" Brown asked his mother. It might have been an indictment, but it wasn't.

"He changed me by having sex," she said.

I worried that this bald statement would embarrass my son, but he just nodded and Seal put her hand on my forearm.

"You don't have to worry, Daddy," she said.

We drove home late that afternoon and then decided to take a walk, just a family out for a stroll on a balmy afternoon. Again we communed rather than discussed, imagined ourselves there together in a war and in collaboration. The sides had not yet been drawn for us. That was probably the best day of my life.

When we got home Rat Man, Rooster, and Reaper were waiting for us at the front door. We greeted them like old friends and invited them into the house.

Brown went upstairs to put on his sweatpants and shirt because his clothes had become too tight. He was both taller and broader—powerful like a warrior instead of an athlete.

While we were busy with the chairs and clothes, Seal talked to the rough men who had meant to do her serious harm only one day before. Dragging two chrome-and-purple vinyl chairs in from the kitchen, Tessa sat down with our daughter and guests. Brown joined them a few moments later while I sought out beer and brandy from the stores of our house.

"I used to go out on Saturday nights lookin' for nigger and beaner asses to kick," Rooster was saying to Brown when I returned. "But now I don't even have anything to say about it. I mean, I don't feel sorry or guilty or anything like that. It just seems silly—stupid, really."

"We killed people, too," Reaper was saying. "Sometimes it was mud people, but we killed just as many of our own when it came to business. It was Lon Farthey that got us jobs and gave the orders."

"He didn't run me, runt," Rooster said.

"Fuck that shit, man. You know you jumped when Raver called. Maybe you grumbled but you still did what he said."

"You want me to come over there and kick your ass, son?"

"You could kiss it, you fat-faced fuck."

"Come on, boys," Rat Man said in an angry yet conciliatory tone. "We didn't come here to fight over Lon."

"Raver," Rooster corrected.

"We need to incapacitate that man who was standing out in the street the other night," I said. "He's very dangerous and the police won't know how to deal with him. He's the one who killed all those people on Hollywood last night."

"We been talkin' about you," Rat Man replied. "You did something to us and we don't even know what it is. The bites have all healed and my mind is like the messy room me and my brother had and then Mama would come in and neaten it all up. Bed made, toys in the closet. We felt real good about a straightened-up room, but it was a mess again in just a few hours."

"And?" I asked.

"We were sure last night about what happened and what to do but we ain't no more. But we still feel different too. It don't feel right. It's like we just don't fit."

"I'm really good at keeping things in order," Temple said with my vocal chords. "Work with me and your bed will be made every night."

"What's wrong with you, man?" spikey-haired Rat Man asked. "I mean, it's like you change into a whole 'nother person."

"I am who I have to be, Mason Drinkman. I can speak your mind or raise the dead, I can clean up the messes you've made and make chocolate milk for us all."

Sitting in the back seat of consciousness, I enjoyed watching Temple orate. He was magnetic and charismatic, as sure of himself as an alpha dog leading a pack of slavering curs in the wilds of India.

"So what is it you want us to do?" Reaper asked.

"I need a hole ten feet deep in the floor of the garage," Temple announced. "That and a heavy-duty freezer that has a storage unit at least six feet long, three feet wide, and two feet deep."

The tattooed white men nodded but made no comment.

Brown glowered and nodded. Celestine completely ignored the request.

"We've been thinkin'," Rooster said.

"Yes?" my template asked.

"We're not on the same page with our boys up in Riverside. Last night we got into fights over what we should and shouldn't be doin'."

"And?"

"We need a place to stay until we get our bearings."

"You'll stay here of course," Seal said. "We'll set up the guest room for two of you and one can stay down here."

Both Temple and I stared at my daughter. She was so certain and upbeat that there was no way to gainsay her offer.

The white men all looked at me.

I, not Temple, said, "Of course you can stay. The work in the garage will take some time and it will be easier to have you here."

"Diggin' a grave for the living dead," Reaper said.

No one commented on this assertion.

"If we're going to have company I'll need to do some shopping," Tessa said sensibly.

"I need to get some clothes, Mom," Brown declared. "If we go to the mall in Century City we can do both."

"I could bake a cake," Seal offered.

My daughter was also changing. She was taller and more womanly—beautiful, as a matter of fact. Her eyes slanted just a bit more and the way she moved was something a father didn't like thinking about.

The white men noticed her.

A father didn't like that either.

It was just then, between levelheaded preparations and parental protectiveness, that the front door flew off its hinges, slamming against the far wall of the foyer. Six armed and partially armored men flooded through the front door while four others appeared from the back rooms. They all carried rifles or shot-guns. These weapons were pointed at us.

"What's going on?" Temple shouted.

"On the floor!" a white man screamed, exhibit-ing a face contorted with rage.

The Aryans and my wife and children obeyed. I wanted to go along but Temple was in charge at that moment.

"What are you doing in my house?"

"On the floor!"

"Fuck you!"

The lead cop slammed me in the head with the butt of his rifle. It was a heavy blow but Temple was both strong and resilient. I was hoping that I didn't have to pay for his bravery with a concussion or worse.

"Hit me with that shit again and I'll take it away from you and shove it up your ass!"

The lead cop was shocked for a moment. He had hit men like this before. They had always fallen into oblivion. He regained his confidence, though, and took a step toward us. Temple pivoted. He had no proper training but in my imagination his body was a weapon and he knew how to hurt and maim and kill.

"Hold it, Faust," came a commanding voice from the front door.

The brutal, enraged cop stopped but I could see that he wanted nothing more than to beat me into a bloody pulp.

Temple smiled at him while I quailed at the back of my own mind.

A hale and tall man in a very nice dark-blue silk suit walked into the living room.

"This is Mr. Just's home," the man explained. "If he wonders why we're here, we should at least answer him."

"Who are you?" Temple asked.

"Captain Short of the Second SWAT team, Hollywood division."

"And why are you here?" I asked, taking the place of my warrior half.

The green moth had plastered itself into a corner of the ceiling. My family and newfound friends were facedown on the floor.

"As you know, Mr. Just, there was a monstrous crime of vehicular homicide committed down on Hollywood Boulevard last night." Short spoke of the tragedy as if he had seen it on television or read about it in some dime novel.

"Yes," I said, "of course. The police came here about it this noon."

"Since a material witness to the crime might have been a Black man," the white captain said, "the officers who questioned you requested that your block be put on the regular officers' route."

"I'm being watched?"

"It's all legal," Captain Short assured me. "These officers noticed three white men loitering around your front door. A closer look told us that these men got into your home. We were worried about your safety. Are you safe?"

"Definitely. These men are new friends."

"Do they have anything to do with the crime you're charged with?"

"You're here about that?"

"All I did was a search on our system. You popped out like a greased pig."

My persona faded into the background and Temple took over.

"You're the pig," Temple informed Captain Short. "I'm the nigger."

This bare statement stopped the good captain for a moment. I think maybe he could see the change in me—maybe not as clearly as one of the Initiated, but he saw some shift in my personality.

"These men are friends of yours?" he asked, waving at the white T-shirts on the floor.

"More than you are."

"What does that mean? You have something against the police?"

"Are you apologizing to me right now?"

"What?"

"Only enemies break down the front and back doors to a man's home. Blackguards shove a man's family facedown on the floor."

"Blackguards? Are you a pirate, Mr. Just?"

"What the fuck do you want with me, man?"

"We came in here to protect you."

"What does that have to do with what happened on Hollywood?" I asked, taking over from Temple. "What does it have to do with my upcoming court date?"

Short could tell that there was some kind of switch going on before him. His eyes narrowed and his head tilted to the left.

"You want we should search them, Captain?" the man who hit me asked.

"Do you want to go outside and talk, Mr. Just?" Captain Short offered.

"No. I want to stay here with my family and my guests."

"It's not necessary, Faust," Captain Short said to my attacker. "We've obviously made a mistake. Mr. Just and his family are not in danger."

"Let's get outta here," Officer Faust said to his men.

Nearly a dozen heavily armed policemen vacated the house in less than a minute.

I followed the captain out onto my front lawn with its lemon trees on one side and its rose bushes on the other.

"What about my door?" I asked the top cop.

"Call my office and give them your name. They'll put you in touch with the people that can reimburse you."

He handed me a card and walked over to a police cruiser while the men from the assault jumped into a very military, canvas-covered flatbed truck.

As the police rolled away I noticed my neighbors, at least two dozen of them, out on the street looking at me and my broken house. Even though I recognized some of them and the others were mostly familiar faces—there was no intimacy between us. My children knew a few of the youngsters on the block. We had hosted some birthday parties but we had no close friends on Charbadon.

Watching my neighbors watching me, I began to understand the moment of development of the Worldmind. This was a philosophical term from German, particularly from Georg Hegel. We, the atoms of life, are separate, alienated from one another, but one day, in a far-flung speculative future, we might unite against the hegemony of matter and antimatter; we might meet in the middle of the street and cleave existence with our meeting.

I was created to stop that assemblage.

"Dad?"

Brown was standing there behind me. Last week, and a thousand years before, he was four inches shorter than I. Now he was half a head taller.

"What?"

"You been standing out here for five minutes."

I looked out again and saw that most of the gawkers had gone back into their houses. Maybe I had stared them down.

"Come on, Dad."

Tessa and Brown went shopping for groceries and clothes for my son. Seal entertained our white guests while I went upstairs to rest my aching crown.

While I slept, Reaper and Rat Man fixed the front and back doors. When Tessa returned, she sat down with Rooster to consider our options. The kids had drifted off like the adolescents they still were. When I finally awoke, Brown was watching television and Celestine was up in her room reading something on the Internet.

"How do we even find this guy?" Rooster was asking.

"Yes," Tessa agreed. "Do you have some way of, of, I don't know . . . feeling him?"

"No," I said. "I don't know . . . maybe. But we don't have to worry. Waxman needs me to make his plans viable. He can kill but he can't raise his victims from the dead without me. If he could capture me then he could build this army of death."

"Then rather than trying to stop him we should be getting you to safety," Tessa said.

"Temple would never let me do that," I proclaimed. "And anyway, Waxman is too dangerous to be allowed to run around free. Everyone he touches will die."

"What do you care?" Rooster asked. "You kill people."

"Only in self-defense."

"If him just touchin' you will kill you, then self-defense should be to run like hell."

"No. He can't hurt any of us. If my virus is transmitted to you first, then it is proof against his."

"I don't even know why I'm here," Rooster complained. He stood up. Maybe he was planning to walk away.

"You're here," Temple said, "because I have made you my vassal."

"Say what?"

This was only the second time that Temple made a statement or did something that was contrary to my own view. When he made love to my wife, I was jealous but I also loved her. When he fought against Lon Farthey (even though I didn't remember it) or when he chased Waxman, I had no disagreement with his actions. Only when he was willing to put innocent lives in jeopardy and now, when he was calling Harold Rimer a slave, did I pull away.

That was exactly what happened—I pulled away. I realized that no matter how strong Temple was, he got that strength from me. If I lost confidence in him, his control over my body abruptly ended.

"Nothing, man," I said, trying to sound like my alter ego. "You're free to do whatever you want. If you want to go and take your friends, I can't hold it against you. Waxman is extremely dangerous but he's my responsibility. I'm going to try to bring him down. I could use your help."

"Why not let the cops do it?" Rooster replied. "They're after him already."

"They don't know what they're dealing with. He could kill thousands before they isolate him. We don't know the extent of his powers. They might not be able to hold him."

126

"I don't really understand what's happening," the big white thug said. "When me and the guys came here yesterday, all we planned to do was bust you up and then kill you and your family. I was mad as hell that you killed Raver. Mad as hell. But then you killed me and brought me back and I remember bein' mad but I don't feel it anymore. I tried a couple'a times to get it back. I still get angry but it's like it's in a box, all locked up except for the shouting. Why is that?"

"I don't really understand," I said honestly. "Waxman and I have . . . missions we are supposed to accomplish. That's why we're here."

"So then shouldn't you two be workin' together?"

"I don't want to work with him. I don't believe in the eradication of life. I don't know what I believe."

We talked for more than an hour while Reaper and Rat Man banged on the doors. The resolution was as it had been in the beginning: we'd dig a ten-foot-deep hole in the garage and get a big freezer for the living corpse of Tor Waxman.

127

*   *   *

"I think you guys should come see this," Brown said when we'd rehashed our lack of strategy for the sixth or seventh time.

Brown was sitting in front of the plasma TV we had installed on the family room wall. A caramel-colored woman with deep-red lips was talking from a seat behind a low desk. I forget her name but she was a news anchor for one of the local stations. Superimposed on the fake wall behind her was the picture of an Asian man wearing a green golfer's hat.

". . . Lee Fung was taken to the hospital for injuries he incurred when he was thrown from his car by the madman who killed twenty-three people on Hollywood Boulevard last night." There was a brief cut to a handheld video of a car ramming through a crowd of pedestrians. Then the scene returned to the brunette anchor. "The doctors said that Mr. Fung's injuries were minor, but just two hours ago his body temperature spiked to one hundred and six and he died before any action could be taken to reduce the fever."

We were all there in the room looking at the news report. There was a video of Lee Fung being carried on a stretcher. He was shaking his head in disgust and talking to a reporter from another news station.

"Doctors are unable to explain what killed Mr. Fung but the police want to add this death to the mounting murder charges against the mad carjacker."

An artist's interpretation of Waxman appeared on the screen. It was an extremely general likeness. There were maybe a thousand men in the city that it resembled.

"It was Waxman," Seal said.

"It's all Waxman," Reaper added. "That man's crazier than any lunatic I ever seen. And I've seen some crazy motherfuckers."

"It's my fault," I said. "If I hadn't, if Temple hadn't chased him, those people would still be alive."

"No," Tessa said with absolute certainty. "The fact that you made his face known will turn the world against him. He would be killing people anyway. That is his nature."

"That's kind of you, baby," I said. "But Temple chased that man. He ran after him with murder in his heart and that's what got all those people killed."

Just then a strain of upbeat staccato music sounded from the TV. A black band appeared across the bottom of the screen carrying red letters that said: **NEWS BULLETIN—THEIR DEATHS RELATING TO THE MAD CARJACKER AND LEE FUNG REPORTED—REDONDO BEACH CALIFORNIA. EIGHTY-ONE KNOWN DEAD.**

The candy-colored news anchor swiveled in her chair to face another camera.

"This just in," she said. "Eighty-four deaths connected with unexplained spiked body temperatures have been reported in the Redondo Beach area.

"For the past week residents of the Redondo Beach Men's Shelter have been reporting to emergency rooms or found dead in their beds or on the street. Most of these men seem to have died of the fever.

"A few days ago, before any illnesses were reported, a man named Troika Meldman took up residence in the area. This man bears a strong resemblance to the artist's picture of the mad carjacker."

The artist's rendition of Tor Waxman once again appeared behind the anchor.

"No one experiencing the illness has survived. The CDC has sent investigators to Redondo Beach and Hollywood to try to come up with some kind of answer to this possible outbreak of some new kind of virus."

"Turn it down, Brown," I said.

All of my family and newfound allies were talking.

"That's crazy," Brown was saying.

"He must be some kind of Typhoid Mary," Rat Man speculated. "He's a carrier, like, and everybody he comes in contact with dies."

"Except us," I said.

"How the hell you expect us to believe that?" Reaper challenged. "I mean, if what you say is true, all he got to do is touch some skin and that's a death sentence."

"You can believe it because I'm saying it," I told Reaper. My voice was absolute in its certainty.

"But you and your family shared blood," Rat Man said.

"They're different but they both hold life," I said. "Waxman will not be able to cross that divide."

There was silence and concern in all our faces. We were stragglers from different military companies and divisions brought together by some great fiasco.

I was in charge but no one had absolute confidence in my ability to lead.

"What should we do?" Tessa asked.

"Start digging that hole. Brown?"

"Yeah, Pop?"

"Help these men dig in the garage. Tessa?"

"Babe?"

"Order that freezer unit online and make sure it's here in a few days."

"What you gonna do?" Rooster asked.

I smiled and Temple did too. We were there at the forefront of consciousness. "We're going to prepare for war," we both said in harmony and yet as one. "Death will come looking for us. He will come at his strongest. He needs me to fuel his foul war. But that will not be."

Everyone's eyes were on me. And I was at peace with my selves and their striations.

War was coming and I was glad.

I was hauled into a meeting with a judge six days later. We met—Lena Clayborn, Fyodor Trapas, Melanie Blythe, me, and a new judge—the Honorable Maxwell Lousange.

The new judge was tall and powerful-looking. He had a strong personality and did not allow my lawyer or the state's attorneys to take over the meeting.

"I don't want a circus in my court, Mr. Trapas," the judge told the prosecutor.

"It's a simple case of manslaughter, your honor. I'm willing to offer eight to fifteen for a plea."

"Ms. Clayborn?" Judge Lousange inquired.

"It's ridiculous, your honor. My client was thrown into a cell with a very large, very violent criminal who had vowed to kill people of color, especially Latinos and African Americans. The guards knew this man's history, at least they should have. My client was found unconscious. There were bruises consistent with strangulation on his throat."

"Your client's knuckles also hit Mr. Farthey's temples so hard that his skull fractured in eight places. That's the coroner's conclusion."

"That may well be," Lena said to the judge, "but if these blows were the reason Mr. Farthey died, then the strangulation had to have happened first. A man with a broken skull cannot strangle another man."

"Mr. Just could have faked the strangulation wounds," Fyodor rebutted.

"Choked himself into unconsciousness to get out of being charged for killing a man in his cell? That's not only farfetched, it's insulting," said Lena.

"He exposed himself to a minor," Trapas added.

"He was walking in his sleep in his own backyard. He had an erection. He was probably looking for a toilet."

Max Lousange had a square face with gray skin lightened here and there by a pink underglow. The judge smiled at my counselor's words.

"Do you have any other evidence, Mr. Trapas?"

"He killed a man with his bare hands, your honor. He subjected a child to a sight that she'll have to carry with her the rest of her life."

"Did he summon the child?"

"Not that we can tell."

"Did he speak to her?"

"No."

"And he was on a deck at the back of his bedroom when he was battered and arrested?"

"Yes, your honor."

"I see that the officers who took Mr. Just into custody suggested that he be put in isolation and seen by a mental health professional."

"The jail was crowded," Trapas argued.

"And Farthey was the only possible cellmate?"

"I can't speak for the officials at the jail facility."

The conversation went on. I stopped listening at some point. I was worried about my family and friends. Waxman was somewhere out there plotting to kill everyone and everything on earth. He needed me to build an army of ambulatory corpses to do his bidding. I had to stop him. These thoughts fanned my impatience with this sham of a pretrial. So what if I murdered someone? All people died in service to the Worldmind. All creatures and organisms, plants, fish, and fowl exist only to add their experience to the advancement of our genes. The tree was my brother as the crocodile is my father. My genes would give rise to living machines that would perfect our qualities and challenge the status quo of existence—there was no time for judgment.

"Can you prove that the killing in the cell was not self-defense?" Lousange was asking Trapas.

"I think that we can mount a convincing argument," the prosecutor claimed.

"This is not a chess game, Mr. Trapas. I'm not interested in circumstantial evidence based more on a sleepwalker's erection than on the fact that the jailers of the city lockup seemed to be trying to put Mr. Just in harm's way. I will not follow that path. Either come to me with proof that Lon Farthey was a victim and not a perpetrator or drop the charges against Mr. Just."

"He killed Lon Farthey," Fyodor Trapas pleaded.

"And Lon Farthey tried to kill him. That evidence is clear."

It had been too long since I'd been home. If something didn't happen soon I was going to start biting people.

"Mr. Just?" the judge said.

"Yes, your honor."

"I can't imagine how a man like you could get into so much trouble in a twelve-hour period. But I fail to see culpability. I'm sorry for your inconvenience."

"That's okay, sir."

"No, sir," the judge said. "It isn't. The police shouldn't have arrested you. The officials at the jail should have put you in isolation. And the prosecutor should have known all this. It is a waste of time for the courts and law enforcement branches to concentrate on law-abiding citizens when real criminals are committing real crimes.

136

"For that reason, I'm asking that the charges against you be dropped and I hope you can pick up the pieces without too much difficulty."

"Just," a man cried as I was heading for the exit, my car, and home.

It was Fyodor Trapas.

I waited for him to catch up to me. He was blowing hard, with hard feelings writ all over his face.

"This is not the end," he warned me.

"No? Did I kill somebody else?"

"You have Farthey's old crew living at your house. That proves a prior knowledge of the victim."

"They came to my place after Farthey was dead. They wanted to express their anger but after a while we came to an understanding and I'm letting them stay with me until they can turn their lives around."

"Horseshit."

"Is there anything else, Mr. Trapas?"

"I'm going to have you in prison, you pervert. I will have you locked up for a very long time."

*   *   *

When I got home everyone was hard at work. The white brotherhood, along with my son, had excavated a deep hole beneath the broken concrete floor of our garage. The coffin-sized freezer had been delivered and Tessa was working to get the proper wiring and conduits needed to keep it running underground.

We bought Seal an iPad, which she used to follow the CDC's investigation of the growing number of fever-related deaths in Southern California. Californians were nearly in a state of panic and the Mad Carjacker was nowhere to be found.

Inside my mind was a continual flipping back and forth of perspective between Temple and me. Whenever Rooster and his men complained or needed direction, Temple took over. I slept in my den because Tessa's sexuality called out to Temple in our bed. Whenever I had the urge to make love to her, he pushed me aside and had at her.

I didn't sleep much at any rate. My deepest fear was being ripped from my body again and flung across the universe, a tissue of nerves and instincts reprogrammed and dropped into a war not of my making.

So in the early hours of the morning, when Temple's persona was quiescent, I'd try to imagine who and what I was, where I was going, and why I was going there.

I couldn't remember a tenth of what I'd known when I woke up after the Annunciation. And what I did remember had little to do with the goals of my actions. I believed that my human sense of understanding was not quite up to the task of interpreting the goals of the Infinite. I had come to believe that the 107 agents and their avatars were like a handful of dice thrown at the world. The outcome would be more a matter of chance than of any actual objective.

"Mr. Just?"

It was the shortest thug, Reaper.

"Yes, Sean?"

"Me and the guys been talkin'. Your boy was out there with us so I figured we might as well let you know."

"What's that?" I asked. Temple was struggling to take over but I resisted him.

"There's five thousand dead by the CDC's numbers and you and me know it could be five times that. This man, this Waxman is a killer like nobody else. And we don't see how or why we should try and stand up against him. I mean, we're all bad men, careless

139

men. We all have done things to get us the death penalty in at least three states. But ever since you did what you did to us, all that is changed."

He paused for a while and then blurted, "I called my mother last night."

"Has it been a long time?" I asked.

"Eleven years."

"Was it good to talk to her?"

"It was like I was distant, you know?" Reaper replied. "Removed. She had a great time talkin' to me. She said she was sorry about the way me and my brother were raised. She asked me to forgive her and I said that I have gotten to a place where I would never had gotten to if she hadn't done what she did. She was happy, but I didn't feel a thing."

"Do you dream, Sean?"

"How did you know?" he asked, searching my face with his cornflower-blue eyes.

"What are your dreams?"

"Life. Trees and fishes, little dust mites crawling on the floor. And all of that comes with the music of the green moth. It's like she's deep in my chest, vibrating like a tuba. I melt down into all that other life and we come up like a soup, a stew of living things that don't care about my mother or brother, friend or foe. We are all in this, like, the same and there's this big shadow wanna crush the life outta us."

I nodded because I had the same dream whenever I managed to doze off.

"And you know, it scares the shit outta me," Reaper said.

"So what do you want to do, Sean?" I asked.

"Me? I wanna go live in the woods somewhere and feel what it's like to just be quiet. I want to let loose'a what I've done, but most of all I want to put some distance between me and Waxman. I don't believe that you or the man that wears your skin from time to time can stand against him. I don't believe it and neither does Rooster or Rat."

"We have eighty-five thousand dollars in the bank," I said by way of an answer.

"Money don't mean nuthin' if you dead or walkin' dead," Reaper said.

"You misunderstand me," I said calmly. "You guys have done a good job with the preparations. I can't ask you to stand up against Waxman. He's a monster and I agree with you—he has a good chance of beating me. Just help us finish with our preparations and I'll take out forty thousand dollars from the bank tomorrow and send you men on your way."

"No joke?"

"I wouldn't fight this battle if I didn't feel I had to," I said.

"You could run with us," Reaper offered.

I had to fight back the urge to cry.

That night I was sitting in the den thinking about Temple making love to my wife. He was forceful and passionate, whereas I always thought about anything I ever did. How does one consider a kiss? In what world does love have words? Temple was a passionate reconfiguration of me. He was a killer without conscience, a lover of any act of a carnal nature. He would lead me like a husky drawing a sled in the middle of an Alaskan winter.

He was the beast of burden but I was in the driver's seat. We didn't like or respect each other but that's what's beautiful about war.

"Dad?"

"Yes, Seal?"

She was standing at the door of my den.

"Come in," I said.

She was wearing the long blue nightgown that I had bought for her not three months before. Then it suited her, but now her womanly figure showed all too clearly beneath its thin fabric.

"I was looking for anything that had to do with people you came across since that day when you were arrested," she said.

"Why?"

"I don't know. It just seemed important. I looked up Lon Farthey, and there's a news report that says his body went missing from the mortuary where his family brought him."

At that moment a dog howled.

Temple moved to the forefront of my mind and I stood back, thinking that Reaper had applied for his liberation one day too late.

One of the systems we had put in place from the second day of our preparations was an alarm set up in every room of the house. Each alarm comprised a flat board and a buzzer powered by four AA batteries. Next to each buzzer was a button. These primitive mechanisms were connected by forty yards of thin yellow wire. Push any button and all the alarms went off at once. I reached for the device but before my finger got there the green moth sent out a shrill warning to every member of our semi-alien tribe.

I pushed the buzzer anyway and went with my daughter to the living room—the prearranged meeting place.

Reaper, Rat Man, and Rooster were already there—barefoot and bright-eyed, frightened and ready for a fight. Tessa and Brown were thundering down the stairs. As they reached the ground floor, a great blow was struck against the front door.

To my pride and surprise the whole group surged forward. Only I, or more accurately my spirit, cringed, moving toward the back of my mind. But Temple led our unlikely band forward. The door was struck again and for the second time in two weeks it came flying off its hinges right at me.

But Temple was up to the challenge. He grabbed the oak plank as easily as if it were made of balsa wood. Through the open doorway, a huge black dog with fever-yellow eyes and a blood-red tongue came loping. Temple slammed the door against the hound, sending the creature tumbling out the front door past a man standing at the threshold.

He was tall with reddish-brown skin and genetically inconsistent silver-colored eyes. I realized that this was Tor Waxman, that the living embodiment of Death could shed bodies one after another, leaving the husk behind to die of fever.

Waxman (he would always be Waxman to me) smiled. Behind him loomed a larger figure who was not yet recognizable.

"I've come for you, Antibody, Cure," the once-Indian man said. "The rest can feed my hound."

The feral beast was once again in the doorway eying us with murderous intent.

"I don't give a fuck about no light-eyed red nigger," Rooster exclaimed.

As the incurable racist stepped forward, Waxman moved to the side, revealing the hulking form of Lon Farthey. The walking corpse wore a soiled hospital gown and a grimace that sent trepidation even through Temple's stout resolve.

Rooster stopped.

"Surprised to see your old friend?" Waxman asked. "It seems that an atom or two of Mr. Just's blood mixed with Lon's after the poor man died of a massive trauma to his brain. I was able to use that iota to make my first servant."

"Hey, boys," Farthey said. His voice was deep and reverbatory, like the voice of a storybook troll calling out from a deep well.

The wolf-sized dog growled and Waxman tittered.

What followed was a span of ten or twelve seconds of absolute peace.

In that time Temple reasserted his resolve and our white allies decided not to run. I could feel my son and daughter and wife standing behind me, ready to give up their lives for my blood in their veins.

"You can switch bodies when you touch your victims," I said to the reincarnation of Waxman. I made this observation to extend the momentary ceasefire. Waxman knew this but took the bait anyway.

"It is one of my abilities," he acknowledged.

"You could work your way through a concert hall in one night," I said. "What do you need with me?"

146

"Even if I killed someone every second," he said with a nod and a smile, "life would surpass me. I couldn't even kill off humanity at that rate, and our goal, as you know, is to end all life on Earth."

"Not my goal," I said.

"Maybe not your wish," he said, now grinning.

At that moment the hound leapt over my head. There was a masculine yell and then a gurgle behind me and I knew one of my allies, possibly even my son, had died. I wanted to turn and kill the dog but Temple was completely in control at that moment. He charged Lon Farthey, surprising the homegrown American killer. I/Temple struck the towering corpse on the edge of his jaw knocking him out the door and onto his back.

"Take Waxman!" Temple yelled at Rooster before jumping at Farthey again.

I was on top of Farthey, throwing punches at his head and torso. He was laughing, counterpunching for every blow I threw. Farthey was so big that it almost seemed as if I were a child play-fighting with his father. We battled like that for maybe half a minute and then he kicked his legs up, throwing me over his head. Landing on my feet and looking into the house, I saw Tessa, Seal, and Rooster trying to hold off Waxman while the black hound was astride my recumbent son, his feral jaws snapping madly. Rat Man and Reaper were both dead on the floor with their throats torn out.

Farthey advanced on me with both hands extended. I remembered then his attempt to strangle me. Temple grabbed him by the wrists and concentrated his will, as if it were a physical thing, against that of the walking corpse.

"You can't hurt me," Farthey said with fetid breath. "I'm already dead."

Temple did not respond.

The hound bit my son on the arm and he yelled. A flash of green sped up from behind, landing on the cur's spine. It was my moth. The next thing I knew the dog yelped and jumped up, trying to bite his own back. The beast pranced up and down, crying and biting. But the moth stuck to his back, humming with a concentration impossible to describe in human terms.

Brown was bleeding and Celestine rushed to help him.

Rooster was leaning up against the wall with a desperate and forlorn look in his eye.

Tessa was holding Waxman back, but just barely. Soon she would succumb to his superior, alien will.

"Uh!" Farthey grunted and I looked back at the man I/Temple was struggling with.

He had fallen to one knee. There was weakness in his face, a look of being frightened like a small child who had lost sight of his mother.

But Temple had no sympathy. "Die again, motherfucker," he hissed.

"No. Please," Farthey begged.

Temple pressed our will forward like it was a battering ram. It entered Farthey's body, and his life force began to dissipate. I felt sorry for the man. I wanted to save him. It seemed to me that my purpose was to save the lives of those poised against me. Life was my only focus, my paramount purpose. Life, I realized, was hope.

Gazing through Temple's eyes, I watched this hope fade for a second time from Lon Farthey's husk. He collapsed and Temple fell to his knees—exhausted.

I forced Temple to look up just in time to see my wife fall to the ground. Waxman, in his new body, pulled out a knife.

Seal yelled.

I pushed Temple's tired persona aside and stood on shaky legs.

"Stop!" I commanded.

Waxman had no choice. He wanted to kill Tessa but my challenge took precedence.

"It's over, Cure," he said with a smile. "I am the superior force. I will always be the victor."

Behind him was the carnage of the attack. The black dog was still hopping, trying to throw off the green moth. Rooster leaned against the wall gibbering to himself, and his friends were dead. Brown was hemorrhaging badly, while Seal tried to stanch the wound.

Waxman was Death and Death is the final movement to any act of life. I knew this but still I staggered forward. Tessa tried to rise but failed. Celestine and Brown watched but neither one of them could help me, involved as they were binding the deep wound in Brown's arm.

I took another step and then bent down to put my hands on my knees.

"Your guardian is depleted," Waxman said. He took a step forward and loomed over me. "You have no hope of standing against me."

His words were as certain as my son's blood. He believed in himself completely.

For a moment then, I gave up hope. All men met this creature sooner or later; even the Powers of Existence ended in the collapse of reality into the primal atom. All things ceased and the only constant was that fact—a certain and final end.

All beings die, I thought. But then I wondered. I was the philosopher in the unaccustomed role of warrior, whose reflex was still the realm of thought.

It occurred to me, bowing there before my executioner, that ever since the beginning, life had not died. There was a spark somewhere a billion or more years ago and the flame of life had risen and raged, waned and sputtered, only to grow once more, spreading across the world. Death had never triumphed over life. I was part of a great conflagration that had kept itself ablaze for ages.

This thought filled my being and the fatigue that had overwhelmed Temple suddenly lifted.

I stood up straight and grabbed Waxman's wrists as Temple had taken hold of Lon Farthey's.

Waxman's new form smiled. "Mortality grabbing onto its own demise for support," he said.

But when I squared my shoulders, his smile thinned.

When my fingers dug into his stolen flesh, he winced.

The hound ran from the house yelping, and somewhere around my diaphragm I found a deep well of strength. It was all the history of Life—not of humanity alone but of the bacteria and insects, dinosaurs and viruses, fish and fowl—all there, all my history and strength.

I looked into Death's visage and saw an empty pit, a place where life rested but did not end. He, Waxman, was little more than the punctuation used to define the long story of Life. I was at the forefront of a living wave and he was only the space through which I progressed.

This knowledge registered in his silver orbs. Fear began to gnaw at the edges of his certainty. He bent forward, seeking to reestablish his superiority. But I was unyielding. I seemed to grow while he remained, as ever, the same. Because Death did not evolve or change, it did not reinvent itself again and again toward ever-elusive perfection. Death was complete in itself and therefore limited to the background. It, Death, was merely a prop for life, a yardstick that measured our advance.

Waxman, the personification of nothingness, saw himself for the first time in the reflective surface of the brilliance of my growing elation. As my power increased, his joints stiffened. His mind grew hazy. His thoughts became senile and repetitive. His lack of life overtook his dreams and he fell to the floor, eyes wide and unseeing, a self-aware corpse unable to manifest even a breath.

I stood there in the necessary carnage of survival. Rat Man and Reaper had had their lives torn from them. Rooster sat on the floor with his back to the wall, moaning at the lies Waxman had imposed on him. My son was bleeding badly. Celestine and Tessa stood on either side of him and were taking him outside, to the car, I supposed.

Waxman was defeated but Death could not die.

"We're taking Brown to the emergency room," Tessa was saying. "Are you all right?"

"Let me help you," I said.

I took a step and fell to my knees.

"You rest," Tessa said. "We'll call from the hospital."

I stayed on my knees for long minutes, panting and reveling in the feeling of a billion years of life behind me.

When I felt the hand on my shoulder I didn't know if that would be the end of my particular branch of existence. It didn't matter. My family was safe. My blood would carry them forward with knowledge that was bound to change the world.

"Is he dead?" Rooster asked in a hollow, haunted tone.

"No. He's paralyzed."

"How'd you do that?"

"I showed him how small and insignificant he was."

Rooster pulled me up by the arm. We stood there facing each other. If we had been different men we would have embraced at that moment.

"He showed me what it was to be dead," Rooster said. "It was a deep trench at the bottom of the ocean—dark and cold and never-ending."

"That's not life, Harold. He wants you to believe it, but it's not true. His masters want it, but once the flame is lit it will never be extinguished."

"We better clean up around here before somebody comes by," Rooster said.

We carried the bodies through the house and out to the garage: Lon "Raver" Farthey, Sean "Reaper" Gardener, Mason "Rat Man" Drinkman, and the tall Indian man who carried the null soul of Tor "Death" Waxman. We plugged in the big white freezer, placed Waxman inside, and were just securing it with thick chains and heavy padlocks when my cell phone sounded.

"Hello?"

"How are you?" Tessa asked.

"Alive. How's Brown?"

"He's going to lose his left arm just below the elbow and he'll be blind in his right eye."

I opened my mouth but there were no words for the grief.

"He told me to tell you that he was okay," Tessa said. "He's going to get the arm replaced with an aluminum bat and he says that that will make him a better soldier in your army."

"I'm so sorry, Tess. I didn't mean to hurt our son like this."

"It's a war, baby," she explained.

"I should have gone after that dog when he jumped over my head. Temple wouldn't let me."

"He was right. If you hadn't stopped that thug Farthey, we'd all be dead now. All but you and I saw in Waxman's thoughts that he would have treated you worse than we plan to do to him."

I watched Rooster tightening the fourth chain around the Death Man's electronic coffin.

"Yeah," I said. "He would have lashed me to a wall in some basement and drained my blood daily to fuel his undead army."

When I shuddered, the green moth flew in, landing on my left shoulder. She purred subliminally and the pain and fear slipped away.

"How's Seal?" I asked.

"She's with her brother. You shouldn't worry, Marty. Sacrifice means survival."

"But he's your son."

"And yours," she said. "He's done us proud, baby. He's done us proud and he's at peace with his wounds. He knows that his loss will give us a chance to succeed."

"Succeed at what?"

"Whatever you decide, Mr. Martin Just. We will follow you even if you die."

"But, but I don't want anybody to die. I just want to live the lives we had last week. You and I getting old together and the kids going to college. They'd give us grandkids and come home for the holidays."

"It's not to be," Tessa said over the radio waves of human technology. I wondered what my blood had whispered to her that I had forgotten.

Rooster and I lowered the big freezer down into the ten-foot grave. The triple-insulated cable that powered it was long enough and we were strong enough, though it was a struggle. We placed the three dead racists into thick plastic bags and, after piling a few feet of dirt on the coffin, we placed them in the grave, both friend and foe. Then we filled the tomb with most of the soil we'd excavated and put the rest behind the house.

In the days to come I would put in a new concrete floor above the burial site. But that night it was enough to lay in the soil.

Tessa and Celestine came home. I made hot chocolate for them and they went up to sleep in my daughter's bedroom. I kissed them goodnight and felt the loss of their leaving.

"That's a beautiful family you have," Rooster said after they were gone.

"You think so?"

"I don't have nobody."

"You don't have any family?"

"No . . . I got blood out there, but ever since that Waxman touched me I knew I was alone. You know, like a boat cut loose to drift out to sea."

"Because you already died," I said, knowing that it was true.

He nodded and said, "I think I'm gonna be movin' on."

"You're welcome to stay, Harold."

"I can't," he replied. "I can hear him down there in the ground. He's callin' to me. And even though I know I wouldn't go there, it would drive me crazy to hear him whisperin'. Maybe if I get far enough away I won't hear it no more."

Not ten minutes later Rooster was walking down the path from my front door to Charbadon Lane. He didn't have so much as a paper bag for luggage.

As he faded into the darkness of the night, I heard the great black dog howl for his master from the nearby hills. One day soon Brown and I would have to hunt the mongrel down and kill him. He was Waxman's familiar as the green moth was mine.

One day we would have to kill that dog, but that night it was enough to hear his baleful cry.